RUDOLF STEINER

ESOTERIC LESSONS FOR THE FIRST CLASS OF THE FREE SCHOOL FOR SPIRITUAL SCIENCE AT THE GOETHEANUM

Volume Two

Lessons Ten through Nineteen

between April 25 and August 2, 1924 in Dornach
for members of the Free School for Spiritual Science

Translated by Frank Thomas Smith

ESOTERIC LESSONS FOR THE FIRST CLASS
OF THE FREE SCHOOL FOR SPIRITUAL SCIENCE AT THE GOETHEANUM

Copyright © 2021 by Anthroposophical Publications,
an Imprint of The e.Lib, Inc.
All Rights Reserved.

No part of this book may be reproduced in any form or by any electronic or mechanical means including information storage and retrieval systems, without permission in writing from the author. The only exception is by a reviewer, who may quote short excerpts in a review.

Cover designed by
James D. Stewart

Rudolf Steiner Portrait by
Peter Gospodinov

For researching these lectures on-line, see GA 241a and GA270:
https://wn.rsarchive.org/Lectures/GA241a/English/eLib2016/FstCl1_index.html
https://wn.rsarchive.org/Lectures/GA270/English/eLib2018a/FstCs1_index.html

Anthroposophical Publications
Visit the website at:
https://anthroposophicalpublications.org/

Printed in the United States of America

ISBN: 978-1-948302-31-9 hard
978-1-948302-30-2 paper
978-1-948302-29-6 eBook

First Printing: November 2021
Anthroposophical Publications

CONTENTS

Lesson Ten 1
Lesson Eleven 15
Lesson Twelve 27
Lesson Thirteen 39
Lesson Fourteen 53
Lesson Fifteen 65
Lesson Sixteen 77
Lesson Seventeen 89
Lesson Eighteen 101
Lesson Nineteen 113

LESSON TEN

Dornach, April 25, 1924

My dear friends,

For esoteric development – the true path to knowledge – the individual must find the way to understanding what it means to live in a world in which the senses, the whole physical organization, in not a facilitator; that is, to live with the psychic-spiritual, which is man's true identity, in a spiritual world. In order to do so there are many different more or less meditative exercises, mental exertions meant to affect the soul.

And to give a picture of what a human soul can pass through on the way from experiencing the physical sensory world to experiencing the spiritual world is what will be provided in these class lessons by means of the various considerations and the summarizing of such considerations in individual verses, which may then be meditated upon according to each member's possibilities and needs.

Once a certain time has passed the communications given in these class lessons, which, as I have often stressed, are real communications from the spiritual world, will coalesce in such a way that those who have participated – it is also karma for those who could be here – will have a complete picture of the first stage of esoteric development.

As a result of the various indications which are given here we can gradually rise above our earthly existence to an experience of the cosmos, we can develop the feelings which carry us out into those distant reaches of the universe from which the spiritual comes to meet us. But as long as we confine ourselves to using our senses and reason only in connection with the sense-perceptible world which surrounds us, it will be impossible for us to grasp what the spiritual world reveals as the truth accessible to man.

You see my dear friends, as I have often stressed, human common sense can understand everything offered by anthroposophy, if it exerts itself sufficiently and is free of prejudice. But it is just in reference to this common sense where a touchstone exists concerning whether or not someone is really destined by their karma nowadays to participate in anthroposophy.

There are two possibilities. One is that the person hears about anthroposophical truths, lets them work on him and considers them to be self-evident. It is obvious that everyone sitting here today belongs to that group. For if someone who does not belong to that group wishes to participate in a lesson as a member, it would not be honest of them. And honesty is the most important aspect of esoteric life – complete truthfulness penetrating the human soul and spirit.

There is another group of people who find what is presented by anthroposophy to be fantastic, somehow belonging only to visionaries. These people show by their behavior that they are not able, according to their karma, to sufficiently separate common sense from physicality and the senses to be able to grasp sense-free truth, sense-free knowledge.

It is therefore the extent to which common sense is bound to corporeality or not which determines such a great divergence between people. For if you honestly consider that you possess a common sense which understands anthroposophy, then at the moment it grasps anthroposophy honestly, it does so independently of corporeality. And this healthy common sense which grasps anthroposophy honestly is the beginning of esoteric striving. And we should treasure the fact that healthy common sense which understands anthroposophy is the beginning of esoteric striving. It should not be overlooked. For when one starts with this understanding through healthy common sense and then follows the indications given in the appropriate schools, one proceeds farther and farther along the esoteric path. You can use whichever of the verses provided here which you consider appropriate for you. But you should apply them together with the indications as to how they relate to the inner life of man.

Today I would like to again provide an indication of how you can leave the body – if only by means of so slight a jolt that you don't even realize it.

We should develop the ability to observe and study the minerals and plants in our environment to the extent that we feel them within – if only by means of thinking – and become truly aware of how this earthly environment is related to us, that due to our wearing a physical body we are directly related to the mineral, vegetable and animal kingdoms around us. And then we ask the question in all honesty: Why? Why did I absorb the physical substances of the earth just by being born? Why do I drag myself through life from birth till death in order to end physical life once my organism is no longer able to process its physical elements? We must deeply feel our relationship to our physical environment starting from such a personal enigma. Then, however, we will also feel more and more what the starting point for esoteric life can be. Then we feel that in physical earthly life we are blindly groping in the dark.

And finally, my dear sisters and brothers, consider the people of today who have been placed in earthly life after birth and educated according to the usual methods and called to this or that work due to purely external circumstances. They do not understand the relationship of this work to the totality of human existence. Perhaps they do not know much more than that they work in order to eat. They do not realize that in the plants they eat cosmic forces from the distant boundaries of the universe are present which pass through the human organism and therefore in a certain sense undergo a cosmic evolution. Many people today cannot even begin to glimpse this process due to the materialism of the times. But to admit that by the mere consideration of earthly relationships one stands spiritually blind in life and lives in the dark – that is the starting point for true esoteric development.

And then change the direction of your gaze from what surrounds you on the earth to the star-studded heaven – either in thought, or if you really want to be affected by it, in reality. Behold the planets, behold the stars, fill yourselves with the infinite transcendence of what shines back to you from the universe, and say to yourself: as human beings we are related just as much to what radiates down from the universe as we are to what surrounds us in the physical environment.

Then by gazing up to the star-studded heaven, we really have the feeling that we do not live in darkness, but that we are freed from life in the darkness by rising with our soul-spiritual being to the stars, rise to what the stars represent as pictures in their constellations. And, you see, if we can really enter meditating into this vision of the star-filled sky it becomes a plenitude of imaginations. You know the old pictures in which not only the constellations have been painted, but in which they have been recapitulated symbolically as animals. Not only the star group that is in Aries, or in Taurus has been represented, but also the symbolic images of the ram and the bull are included.

Today people think: Well, it was arbitrary on the part of those ancient inhabitants of the earth that just because the constellations were so named that the corresponding pictures were added. But that was not the case at all. In reality in ancient times the shepherds in the fields did not merely gaze up at the star-studded sky with physical eyes, but also in dream-consciousness or sleep-consciousness out there with their flocks they turned their souls with closed eyes towards outer space. They did not see the constellations which physical eyes see. But they actually perceived those pictures, those imaginations which fill universal space – albeit somewhat differently from what was later painted.

We can no longer go back to what the simple shepherds experienced by instinctive clairvoyance. But we can do something else. With far greater thoughtfulness we can imagine ourselves into the star-filled sky. We can feel the depth and at the same time the awesome majesty of what radiates back to us. And gradually we can come to a sense of veneration for what is expanding out there in cosmic space. And the more ardent the veneration is the more clearly can the experience be that the outer sense-images of the stars disappear and the star-filled sky becomes an Imagination for us. But only then, when the star-filled sky becomes an Imagination for us, do we feel ourselves carried away by our soul's vision.

You see, still in Plato's time one felt something special about the physical eye when it is observing. Plato himself described seeing as follows: When I look at a person something leaves my eye and encompasses him. People in ancient times sensed that something streams out of the eye and encompasses the object. The etheric streams out. Just as when I stretch out my hand and grasp something I know that I am connected to my hand until reaching the grasped object, so in the times of instinctive clairvoyance people knew that something etheric goes out from the eye and encompasses the thing looked at. Today people think, well, the eye is here, the object seen is there. So the object sends out ether-waves which drum against the eye and the drumming is perceived by some kind of soul – about which even the materialist talks about here, but without having any idea of what it is. But that is not true. It is not a mere impact on the person emanating from the object, but really also an emanation of the person's inner etheric substance.

And we perceive our ether body as belonging to the universe when the star-filled sky becomes for us the grand open page of the universe on which the imaginative secrets of cosmic being are written — if we are able to read it.

And then the feeling comes to us: When you are here on earth you are in the robust sense-perceptible reality. But you are blind, you live in darkness. When you rise up with your sensibility then you live in what otherwise only shines down to you from the distant universe, and you live in the illusion of the distant universe. But at the same time you take your own etheric being out into the distant flooding stream of this illusionary world.

And the illusion ceases to be illusion. It cannot be a nothing if we immerse ourselves in it. When we have this feeling — I will draw it —.

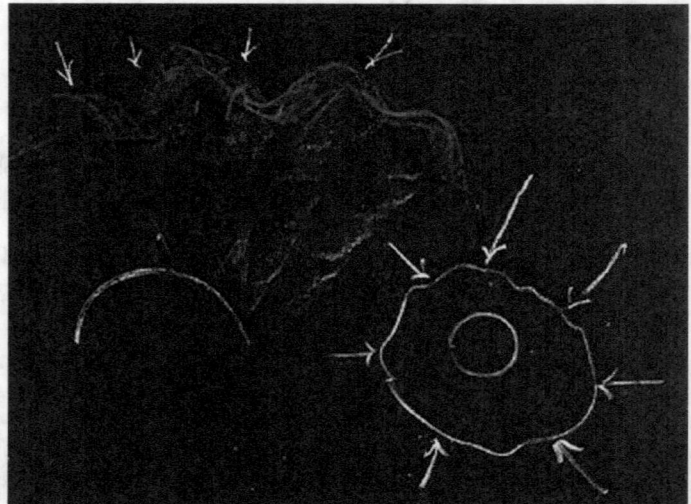

Blackboard Drawing For Lesson Ten

We live as blind people in the darkness of earthly existence, [white arc]; then we journey out into the distant universe [yellow rays], at the end of which we can feel the cosmic Imaginations by means of reverence for the brilliance of the stars [red waves].

So now that we have journeyed out we are together with our etheric being within the imaginative cosmic web. If we can accomplish this, then we are no longer in the physical body. We have traveled through the etheric emptiness to experiencing the cosmic Imaginations.

You see, it's like when in the physical world someone writes something down and, because we have learned to read, we read it. By being out in the cosmos — the gods have written the cosmic imaginations for us in the cosmos — when we arrive we see the imaginations from the other side [arrows]. At first we live here on the earth [inner circle]. Then we draw ourselves up to the cosmic imaginations [outer wave-circle].

Yes, my dear friends, my sisters and brothers, the zodiac speaks a meaningful language when we do not observe it from the earth – Arias, Taurus, Gemini, Cancer, Leo – but rather when we encircle it from without. And it is a task of our consciousness to encircle it from without. Then we begin to read the cosmic secrets, which are the deeds of the spiritual beings. In a novel we read of the deeds of men. When we look at the zodiac from the other side and read what from the earth we see virtually from behind, as Moses was told that he always had to look at God from behind, that is, from the earth. Initiation consists of seeing from the other side – not a matter of gawking, but of reading. And what we read are the spiritual deeds of the spiritual beings who brought it all about.

And when we have silently read long enough, when our souls have concentrated deeply on this reading, then we begin to hear in a spiritual way. Then the gods speak with us. When the gods speak with us we are within the spiritual world.

Now you see, my dear sisters and brothers, the initiate can tell you: the soul can rise up to the cosmic heights, receive the cosmic imaginations, read them from the other side, the spiritual deeds, become capable of hearing in a spiritual way the language of the gods.

But if you really immerse yourself in what the initiate relates with your whole heart, your whole feeling, if you don't just listen to it greedily and say: Well, if I also could do that I'd like it, it would be interesting – but I'm not going to bother. But you receive it as something which you can revere, which you can love, which you can repeatedly meditate on, then it is the path to enter esoteric life yourself.

And you will find this path by meditating profoundly on the words:

[The first part of the verse is written on the blackboard.]

1. *I live in the dark domain of the earth,*

2. *I wander in the brilliance of the stars,*

3. *I read in the deeds of the spirits.*

4. *I hear in the speech of the gods.*

When experienced with the necessary deeply meditative feeling this works wonders in the human soul, transforms the human soul. It must rhythmically flow through the soul again and again, for it leads the human being through his own interior cosmic being.

But it is necessary that such a thing be deeply internalized. And even though it still speaks more to the head, the heart should also participate in the whole process of going out into the etheric universe, then into the spiritual universe, that is, on the other side of the universe. It is necessary in such a process that we take our hearts with us in the experience and that it stimulate in you the feelings which can come quite naturally by this excursion into the outer universe. But these feelings must be really stimulated. It is therefore good the look deeply into what the words say:

I live in the dark domain of the earth,

I wander in the brilliance of the stars,

I read in the deeds of the spirits.

I hear in the speech of the gods.

Then you try to imagine that someone is speaking to you from a spiritual depth, as though you were not thinking it, but as though you were hearing it, as if another being were speaking. You really imagine that another being is speaking to you from an unknown depth. Then you try to develop the right feelings for what you have heard.

These feelings live in the second part of the verse:

[The second part is written on the blackboard.]

5 *The darkness of the earth creates longing in me,*

6 *The brilliance of the stars is comfort to me.*

When I am aware that I live blindly in the darkness of the earth, I long to get out. Then the brilliance of the stars becomes the comforter which expands my being:

The brilliance of the stars is comfort to me.

Now from the other side:

7 *The deeds of the spirits are teaching to me,*

— when I read them —

8 *The speech of the gods is creating to me.*

Only you must use it correctly. Imagine yourself vividly in this meditating which you are doing. As though someone were speaking to you from spiritual depths is how you hear the lines of the first verse. You bring the corresponding feeling to each verse, so that you experience in the meditation: first listen, then bring feeling; listen, then bring feeling; and so on.

[An arc is drawn connecting lines 1 and 5; another connecting 2 and 6; another connecting 3 and 7, and another connecting lines 4 and 8:]

[1] I live in the dark domain of the earth,

((*The earth's darkness extinguishes me.*

[5] The darkness of the earth creates longing in me,

[2] I wander in the brilliance of the stars,

((*The brilliance of the stars awakens me.*

[6[The brilliance of the stars is comfort to me.

[3] I read in the deeds of the spirits,

((*The deeds of the spirits call to me.*

[7] The deeds of the spirits are teaching to me.

[4[I hear in the speech of the gods,

((*The speech of the gods engenders me.*

[8] The speech of the gods is creating for me.

It is a meditation in dialog in which you always objectify the first line, but the second you feel as though streaming out of your heart.

Now you try again to visualize how one acts and weaves into the other, and then try to feel with your will what you can experience through the dialog.

[The third part of the verse is arranged in connection with the first and the second parts while lines 9, 10, 11 and 12 are written on the blackboard.]

From depth of spirit resounds:

I live in the dark domain of the earth,

The heart replies:

The darkness of the earth creates longing in me.

The will senses the impulse in the dialog between lines 1 and 5:

9 The earth's darkness extinguishes me.

After this dialog has taken place we recall the connection of lines 2 and 6:

I wander in the brilliance of the stars,
The brilliance of the stars is comfort to me.

10 The brilliance of the stars awakens me.

Afterward we recall what resounds from spiritual depths and the heart's reply:

I read in the deeds of the spirits,
The deeds of the spirits are teaching to me.

The will now senses:

11 The deeds of the spirits call to me.
(into the spiritual world.)

And now the most sublime, where we feel ourselves in dialog with the gods themselves, where the gods not only let us read, but speak:

I hear in the speech of the gods,
The speech of the gods is creating for me.

12 The speech of the gods engenders me.
(brings me forth, engenders me.)

Now imagine the whole meditation. It runs as follows: dialog – line for line with a spiritual being present in the dim spiritual depths that always speaks the top line of the verse. And the heart always replies:

I live in the dark domain of the earth,

The darkness of the earth creates longing in me,

I wander in the brilliance of the stars,

The brilliance of the stars is comfort to me,

I read in the deeds of the spirits,

The deeds of the spirits are teaching to me,

I hear in the speech of the gods,

The speech of the gods is creating for me,

Now I recall each one and add the outpouring of will as a remembrance of what had just gone before:

I live in the dark domain of the earth,

The darkness of the earth creates longing in me,

The earth's darkness extinguishes me.

I wander in the brilliance of the stars,

The brilliance of the stars is comfort to me,

The brilliance of the stars awakens me.

I read in the deeds of the spirits,

The deeds of the spirits are teaching to me,

The deeds of the spirits call to me.

I hear in the speech of the gods,

The speech of the gods is creating for me,

The speech of the gods engenders me.

Conviction results from the dialog in meditation, from recalling the dialog and in strengthening the recollection by means of the will.

If, firstly, with inner devotional feeling, secondly with complete soul and interest we have done what I have just described, if we do it not as mechanical meditating but as a true experience of the soul, then this means of creating a relation to the spiritual world really does have an awakening effect on the soul.

Also in the case of the last verse, which in the way I have described should really be experienced as remembrance of speech and answering speech — speech of the spirit and answering speech of the heart, we must correctly feel how, firstly, consciousness, which we wish to achieve, is extinguished by the earth's darkness. We must sense how a moment of extinguishing sleep overcomes consciousness, and how upon awakening, at the second line, we hear the spirits calling us to them, how afterward we feel: the spirits have called us so that they can bring us forth, engender us in the spiritual world by their own cosmic word.

If these nuances of inner experience flow through the soul — and the representations of the spiritual being who speaks to us are included — and the heart reciprocates with its dedication to the spiritual being, then yes, then the stimulation exists in the soul which will gradually lead this soul onto the esoteric path. And we must be clear that as we experience these three verses in our souls in the way in which I have described as best we can, something powerful takes place in the subconscious mind. If we sincerely live in these three verses as I have described, then when the first line resounds, our soul unconsciously passes through the starting-point of earthly life when the etheric body was first formed.

If we can vividly imagine what from the spirit resounds:

I live in the dark domain of the earth,

we approach — in the unconscious — with this hearing in spirit, the moment in which our etheric body was formed; and from pre-earthly existence, from life between death and a new birth, acts the force with which we sincerely reply from the heart:

The darkness of the earth creates longing in me;

because we have the longing for the spiritual as a heritage from pre-earthly existence.

And again we are transported to the beginning of earthly existence. And what acts from our hearts is inspired by the previous earthly existence.

I wander in the brilliance of the stars:

transported to the beginning of our earthly life.

The real comfort the brilliance of the stars can give when we are transported back is in our heart's reply:

The brilliance of the stars is comfort to me.

I read in the deeds of the spirits:

transported back to the earth's beginning,

and remember how we are taught by spiritual beings in pre-earthly existence.

The deeds of the spirits are teaching to me,

among whom I lived and wandered before I descended to the earth.

I hear in the speech of the gods:

We heard them during the period between death and a new birth. We sense that what the gods say is not mere information as is what men say; we realize that the speech of the Gods is creative:

The speech of the gods is creating for me.

But then, if we can see it so, lines 9, 10, 11, 12 also acquire the correct meaning:

[Line 9 is written again, this time on the arc connecting lines 1 and 5.]

The earth's darkness extinguishes me,

removes me from my present earth life for I am led back, through the region between death and a new birth, to my earlier incarnation. I divine this; therefor my consciousness is extinguished, for my consciousness was, until now, that of my current incarnation. In this moment of sleep I am transported back so I can divine: I am wandering in my previous incarnation.

I wander in the brilliance of the stars,

The brilliance of the stars is comfort to me,

[Line 10 is written again, this time at the arc connecting lines 2 and 6.]

The brilliance of the stars awakens me.

I am brought back to what I was in the previous incarnation as though awakened in it. My karma arises before me, the connection of destiny arises before me, it arises before me from the other side.

I read in the deeds of the spirits,

The deeds of the spirits are teaching to me,

[Line 11 is written again, at the arc connecting lines 3 and 7.]

The deeds of the spirits call to me

to fulfill my karma with the forces which derive from my previous earth-life.

I hear in the speech of the gods,

The speech of the gods is creating for me,

[Line 12 is written again, at the arc connecting lines 4 and 8.]

The speech of the gods engenders me.

Everything I am becomes clear to me when my earlier earthly existence penetrates the present one and shines through it and wanders through it and pulses through it. For here I am. My present I is in a process, it is a seed which will have meaning once I have passed through the gates of death. What shines and works in me from the previous earthly existence into the present one makes me into a human being, engenders me as an existing human being.

If we have the conviction that it is so, that – although we believe only to be in the ordinary world of physical existence – our soul really makes the journey back to the previous earth-life, then we will be aware of the gravity of what we are experiencing. And through this awareness a warmer, luminous current streams through our thinking, feeling and willing. And with that inner magical feeling, which is necessary for the meditation to work in the right way, our meditation will prevail. We may call it a magical feeling for it cannot be compared with any feeling we have on earth, because it is completely independent of all corporeality. If we cannot yet leave the physical body behind with our thinking, this magical thinking which we experience through the gravity of our soul's activity is present in the purely spiritual world.

According to the way we experience these things, our esoteric striving is fulfilled. And that is what I was obliged to lay before your souls today, my dear sisters and brothers.

———

In conclusion I would like to say one more thing. It should not happen that someone passes on the verses and the information given here without first asking permission. Only with permission may these things be passed on from one to another or to a group. It is especially frowned upon, my dear friends, that these verses or their interpretation be sent by post. They may not be sent by post, and I ask that this be strictly observed.

LESSON ELEVEN

Dornach, May 2, 1924

My dear friends,

You have all probably been deeply affected this morning by the news that Miss Maryon*[1] has departed from the physical plane – although it is something long expected and which follows difficult suffering which lasted more than a year.

Tomorrow when the members of the Anthroposophical Society are all gathered here, I will say what I have to say about Miss Maryon's departure from the physical plane. For now it is sufficient to say that the First Class has lost a truly dedicated student, for among those who have devoted themselves to the School with great diligence, Miss Maryon was the best. Despite the serious illness which afflicted her she not only participated in what is being esoterically developed here, but she also let the exercises given here work on her and lived with them in an extraordinarily intimate way.

This was the result of her having been familiar with esotericism before coming to us. She belonged to an esoteric school of a completely different nature before she discovered the Anthroposophical Society and through this esoteric school made the complete transition to Anthroposophy quickly. The esoteric was essential to her and she experienced it intensely during the years with us on the physical plane. She has departed from the physical plane but certainly not from Anthroposophy.

It would be unseemly to say more now as she has just left the physical plane. Tomorrow, though, when the members, the friends are here, it will be my task to say what is to be said.

———

My dear friends, in esoteric striving it is necessary to at least envision, to the extent possible, the path upon which real knowledge of spiritual things can be realized. Of course how far one or the other comes along this path depends on his karma, on what conditions he brings along from previous earth lives.

But not only that, it also depends on which physical and environmental conditions the person's destiny places him. Much old karmic residue may exist to be worked out which hinders achieving everything which is otherwise within one's capabilities. Thus

---

[1] Miss Maryon: **Edith Louisa Maryon** (London, 9 February 1872 – 2 May 1924 in Dornach, Switzerland) was an English sculptor. She belonged to the innermost circle of founders of Anthroposophy and those around Rudolf Steiner. Maryon met Rudolf Steiner in 1912/13 and after the summer of 1914 she moved to Dornach. She worked with Steiner on the construction of the first Goetheanum, where she along with Steiner worked on the sculpture *The Representative of Humanity*. She served as the head of the Section of Fine Arts at the Goetheanum. She died of tuberculosis.

much which perhaps could be quickly achieved without these karmic residues takes longer.

My dear sisters and brothers, we should never give up hope, never lose patience or energy, but continue on our way. When the right time has come, we will surely find what has been predestined. For certain lines of every human being's life path are uniquely predestined despite or perhaps because of freedom. Every individual is called to his life's task and can accomplish it with sufficient good will.

Here in this Free School for Spiritual Science everything that existed in the Mysteries in the past when they especially flowered is to be reenacted in the correct form according to our time and to the future. The flowering time of the Mysteries had already passed when the greatest Mystery of all, the one most hidden to world history, took place: the Mystery of Golgotha. After their flowering time, the Mysteries declined, a process in which, just because the Mysteries had declined, humanity could be taken into the stream of world evolution where freedom is possible.

Nevertheless, the time has now come when the Mysteries are to be renewed, in the fullest sense of the word and in the appropriate form. And once these things have been thought about correctly in the future the Goetheanum's work will be appreciated in the world, because the task of this Goetheanum is to renew the Mysteries. And only, my dear sisters and brothers, if we are permeated with the will to understand this School as representing, through us, a renewal of the Mysteries, can we participate in the Mysteries and in the School in the right way.

If you will remember what was presented here in the last Lesson, then what I have just said can live in your hearts. For the transition is made in meditation to really enter directly into the individual's experience so that he frees himself from the narrow limits of his personality.

In the triple-versed structure of the last meditation we saw how we place ourselves in the world process and how in the meditation we confront not only what resounds from our soul but also what resounds *to* our soul, which in a certain way incorporates itself into a general universal language, a general universal Word. But only when the individual gradually frees himself from the limits of his personality, when he finds himself meditating in an ever more objective way, then will he be able to follow that intimate, subtle path, which is the true path to human knowledge. But for this to happen the objective truths which apply to humanity must become objectively present in him in the most varied ways.

You all know, my dear sisters and brothers, what has often been described as the threefold human nature: the nerve-sensory man, mostly represented by the human head; the rhythmic man, mostly represented by the breast, in which the respiratory and circulatory organs are concentrated. All these organs are everywhere in the organism, are located in other parts of the body as well, but more in certain areas than in others. Then we have the limbs-metabolism-organization, localized downward and outward.

That which can be known theoretically can also be meditatively objective. And when it is meditatively objective it becomes esoteric. Therefore in meditation we must intensively and intimately keep this threefold man in view.

So we have the head-organization, a real replica of the entire cosmos. We have the breast or rhythmic organization, which does not directly show in its form the cosmic image. And least of all does the limbs-metabolism-organization show the image of the cosmos. But man must be intimately conscious of how he places himself in the cosmos through each of these organizations. He must be clear about what takes place in his head. We can feel this directly: when we think, our head is active. We notice that when the head is ailing, thinking is impaired. We sense the head's association to this clearest human earthly activity in both normal and abnormal circumstances. This doesn't mean that the head is really the bearer of the clearest human earthly activity, but it seems so to us.

What is actually going on? When do we see ourselves – in our heads – in the right way? Only, my dear sisters and brothers, when we are aware that this human head would not exist if the star-filled sky did not arch above us. For the moment we will not dispute what the astronomers say about this; we are only taking into account what is visible to the eyes: the sublime starry heavens.

In the previous lesson much was said about this. The stars are there above; their rays of light approach us when we look up at them. But they don't only approach us, we also receive them. And what we receive of the rays of light we enclose in our heads. And out of it sprouts our human activity on earth: our thinking. And so we must imagine: Outside are the stars; our heads receive the effects of the stars' rays. From without it looks as though the stars were sending their rays down to us. Our heads receive these rays; so what has been received is within our heads. From here is looks quite different than from without, but it is the same, the whole starry sky rolled together, so to speak, within our heads.

But only the starry sky? No, not only the starry sky. For – what are the stars? What is in the individual stars which rays toward us? It is the domicile of the gods. They are the places where the gods reside. It is where the gods were sought in the times when instinctive clairvoyance knew where the gods reside, which are the places worthy of the gods.

During the times when such clairvoyance existed, people did not look up at burning points in the cosmos, but at the dwelling places of the gods. And in doing so had a truer idea of what exists in the far reaches of space than do the astronomers of today who observe the points of light and calculate their positions and angles to each other.

But in that man is a threefold being, he speaks and acts through what holds him together: his I – through all three elements of his being, through the nerve-sensory-system, the head; through the rhythmic system, the breast; and through the metabolic-limbs-system. It is held together only because the physical body is a unity. But man always sends his I into the three individual elements and we will learn today the different ways he sends this I into the individual elements.

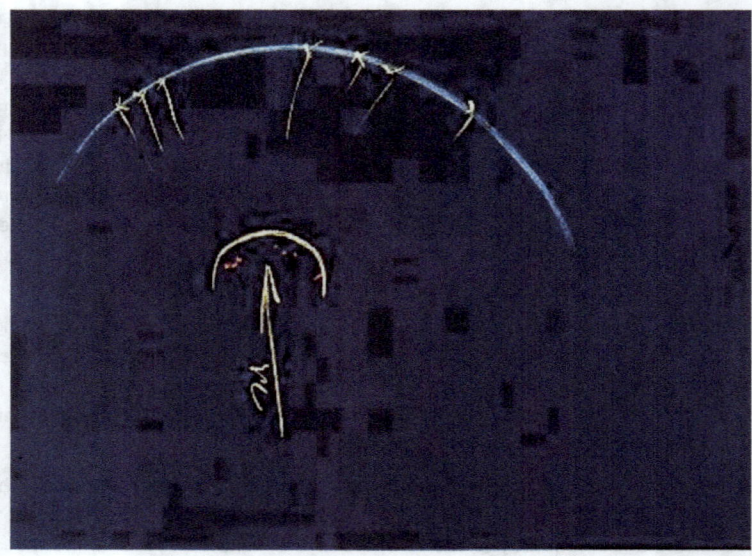

Blackboard Drawing for Lesson Eleven

At first man speaks the I through his thoughts into his head from his innermost being. Truly, it is thus: [draws on the blackboard]: What unfolds without as the shining element of the stars [blue arc, yellow stars], acts in the human head [yellow arc and rays from the stars]. It is also here within [red dots]. Man speaks his I from out of his center of his being into this rolled together cosmic space which is the interior of his head [arrow with the word "Ich", yellow]. And he should become aware that when he speaks his I into the part of his humanity which is an image of the dwellings of the gods, then the gods themselves who live in these dwellings will act in him. We meditate correctly when we are aware that when we say "I" through the force of our heads, the gods of cosmic space and cosmic time speak in us.

And this is not a teaching given to us on the earth; it is a teaching, my dear sisters and brothers, given to us by the beings of the higher hierarchies themselves, at first from those beings who are with us humans: the Angeloi, and in the background the directing Archangeloi. This element of human nature – this I – has a relation to the dwelling places of the gods in the radiant stars, from out of which the godly beings themselves speak, and should let itself be taught by the beings we have always referred to as Angeloi in our descriptions of the hierarchies.

We correctly accomplish a meditation thus: We look up, allowing ourselves to be impressed by the radiance of the stars, sense that cosmic space itself is sending us words. And these words should be:

Starry-cosmic-spaces,
Dwellings-of-the-gods!

It resounds in the periphery. Thus we imagine that we hear it from cosmic space.

Starry-cosmic-spaces,
Dwellings-of-the-gods!

It becomes an echo in us. We treat it as a call, but a call that excites us, because all heaven resounds in this call. This is how we meditate. And then we will be conscious of what we have to say from the depths of our souls, from whence in the stillness we answer the cosmic trumpet-call:

When human-spirit-radiance
Says in head-held-high
The "I am":

That is what we say. Then the angel who belongs to us answers in our meditation:

Thus you live
– the gods –

in the earth-body
as a human being.

That is the sense of this meditation. We hear it as a world-spanning trumpet call from all sides:

Starry-cosmic-spaces,
Dwellings-of-the-gods!

We answer in stillness intimately praying:

When human-spirit-radiance
Speaks in head held high
The "I am":

The angel answers, looking upward to the source of the trumpet call:

Thus you live in the earth-body
as a human being.

And we accept these last two lines which the angel speaks in our meditation as a teaching.

[The first verse is written on the blackboard.]

*Starry-cosmic-spaces,
Dwellings-of-the-gods!
When human-spirit-radiance
Speaks in the head held high*

— the scrolled together starry radiance, the human radiance —

The "I am" :

The spiritual teacher Angelos:

*Thus you live in the earth-body
as a human being.*

— Starry-cosmic-spaces, Dwellings-of-the-gods! —

That is the first dialog with the cosmos and with the third hierarchy. Seen this way it is a deeply penetrating meditation on the human spirit, human soul and human body.

Now we go further to the rhythmic organization of man. We think of the lungs and the heart, the wonderful pulsation, the rhythm of breathing which by its very nature reveals that it is the expression of the deepest cosmic laws, the movement of which we sense in us. When we concentrate in meditation on our head, we sense rest. When we meditate on our breast, we feel movement. And this movement is an image of the movement of the planets, of the moon, the sun, of Mars, Mercury, Jupiter, Venus, Saturn. But a representative of this movement is the sun. It is closest to us. Every day it circles around our earth — in appearance. It can therefore stand as representative. But just as we carry within us the starry-cosmic-spaces, dwellings-of-the-gods, rolled together, so also the movements of the whole planetary system — represented by the sun — in our breathing, in our blood circulation, in everything which is movement in our organism.

Therefore we must imagine that just as the sublimity of the dwellings-of-the-gods was announced by the trumpet calls from all sides of the cosmos, also what the movements of the planets, represented by the sun, have to say through melodious sound courses through our bodies:

Cosmic sun circling
Paths of spirits acting!

That is the second thing: stillness in comparison to the loud trumpet-call of the cosmic surroundings.

Starry-cosmic- spaces,
Dwellings-of-the-gods!

It resounds majestically from all sides. That is what we must meditate on. But following on the path of the sun and the other planets in our breathing and in our blood circulation it resounds joyfully within us:

Cosmic sun circling
Paths of spirits acting!

Now we say intimately from within us, if we take as inducement what resounds melodiously from the star-circles into our own bodies:

Resound in heart's center
Human-soul-weaving
The "I live":

The Angelos replies, speaking to the gods in the circling planets:

So you stride in earth's course
As humanity's creative force.

Just as the human being lives on the earth by means of what radiates into him from the dwellings of the gods, so does the human creative evolutionary force live by means of the activity of the gods in the planets' movements, which is also received into man's rhythmic system. Thus we have again the threefold verse: objective murmur through our body in the sense of the planets' course; our own intimate speech; the Angelos' reply:

Cosmic sun circling
Paths of spirits acting!
Resound in heart's center
Human-soul-weaving
The "I live":
Thus you stride in earth's course
As humanity's creative force.

[These lines are now written on the blackboard.]

Cosmic sun circling,
Paths of spirits acting!
Resound in heart's center.

- above "<u>speaks</u>", here "<u>resounds</u>"; above "head-held-<u>high</u>"; here "heart's <u>center</u>" -

Human-soul-weaving
The "I live":

– above "I <u>am</u>"; here "I <u>live</u>" –

Thus you stride in earth's course
As humanity's creative force.

Each of these verses must be felt as being threefold in their coming into being: The objective resounding; our own intimate speech as the echo within us; the speech of the Angelos. Then it works correctly in us.

However, when we come to the third element of man – what lives in the arms and legs and continues inward in metabolism – then we do not hear the trumpet calls from the cosmos, then we do not hear the melodiousness of the planets, then we hear the dull rumbling of the world-foundation itself. It is what makes us earth-people. The limbs do not participate in our spiritual being. They are completely shaped according to the earthly forces: the arms and hands are only partly shaped by the air forces, but otherwise all is shaped by the forces that arise from out of the cosmic foundations and flow up through human beings. We must be conscious of this. Just as we hear in the first verse the language of the cosmos itself in the majestic tones coming from the cosmic periphery, as we hear the speech of the periphery in the second verse, we hear the rumbling speech of cosmic foundation from the depths of the earth in the third verse:

Cosmic-foundation-powers,

Creator's luster of love!

It is not a luster of light, it is a luster of love. For in those places where otherwise what is in the periphery is gathered in the center is where the source of the love-forces also lie. Therefore we cannot answer in echo "speaks" and also not "resounds", here we must answer with the deed, with what flows from the will. We must not "speak", not "resound", here we must "create". Therefore we answer from within pouring will into our words:

Create in the body's limbs
Human-action-streams
The "I will":

Then the angel answers in that he lowers his eyes to what is rumbling from the cosmic-foundations – "rumbling" not in an antipathetic sense, but only in the dullness of the tone – the active forces answer which resound in the cosmic-foundation's depths:

Thus do you strive in earthly works
as human sensory deeds.

Again the threefold verse:

Cosmic-foundation-powers,
Creator's luster of love!

Create in the body's limbs
Human-action-streams
The "I will":
Thus do you strive in earthly works
as human sensory deeds.

[This third verse is written on the blackboard.]

> *Cosmic-foundation-powers,*
> *Creator's luster of love!*
> <u>*Creates*</u> *in the body's limbs*

– "speaks", "resounds", "creates" – [creates is underlined.]

– "height". "center", "limbs", what strives from the center outwards – ["limbs" is underlined.]

Human-action-streams
The "I <u>will</u>":

– "I am", "live", "will" – ["will" is underlined.]

Thus do you strive in earthly works

– "<u>*earthly-body*</u>", <u>*Earthly-path*</u>, <u>*earthly-works*</u>" [the three words are underlined.]

as human sensory deeds.

– "being", "creative force", "sensory deeds", which means: deeds visible to the senses – [the three words in quotation marks are underlined.]

True meditation, true exercise of the soul is not found in the theoretical, intellectual content of a meditation verse, but in its mantric character. The mantric character is present when the meaning dissolves into situation and happening and when we free ourselves from the theoretical, from the intellectual content, go out from ourselves, so that we do not merely have something vague in our thoughts, but have the idea that the sky, that the periphery, that the earthly depths resound; that we reply to these sounds from our own intimate inner self; that the angel interprets and teaches.

We should try to attain such an ideal setting, that is, to make meditation something in which we don't merely think, feel or will, but which also streams and weaves and radiates around us, and from all this something steps back into the life of the heart and in the heart it is streaming, weaving, striving and vibrantly radiating so that we feel ourselves integrated in the life of the world, of the cosmos, so that our meditation is not something that only lives in us, in our feeling, but which lives in us and the world; it extinguishes the world, extinguishes us, and in extinguishing unites us and the world, so that we can just as easily say: "The world is speaking" as we can say "We are speaking". This gradually enhances the character of the meditation.

If the meditation is practiced in this way, — by extinguishing what has always seemed to be one's ordinary self – it is possible to perceive oneself as spirit.

When, however, we start along this path of knowledge, when we honestly approach such paths of knowledge, we learn that we are not alone in the world, that we are in a dialog with the spiritual world, and through this we approach closer and closer to a renewal of the Mysteries. Of course physical, outer temples stood in places on the earth which today are considered to be uncivilized. Outer temples stood there, and early peoples needed outer temples. But these temples were not the only ones, not even the most important ones. For the most important temples have no place, have no time. One comes to them if one exercises the soul in the way that has been indicated here and in the Mysteries of all times.

In order to be clear, my dear sisters and brothers, if we live in such a mantric formula, it is thus:

Here I stand – each of us says rightly – and all around me is the everyday world. Bourgeois walls and chairs are around me, or perhaps a natural forest, visible trees, or houses. It is all there. I am fully aware that this is my environment; it is there and I see and touch it. But the meditation arises in my soul while I am in the external, sensory world. The meditation arises in me:

> Starry-cosmic-spaces,
> Dwellings-of-the-gods!
> When human-spirit-radiance
> Speaks in head-held-high
> The "I am" :
> Thus you live in an earthly body
> Now as a human being.

> Welten-Sternen-Stätten,
> Götter-Heimat-Orte!
> Spricht in Hauptheshöhe
> Menschen-Geistes-Strahlung
> Das "Ich bin":
> So lebt Ihr im Erdenleibe
> Als Menschen-Wesenheit.

What do I sense moving? What do I sense arching over me? It is something; it is nothing. I sense walls, I don't see them.
The meditation continues:

> Cosmic sun circles
> Paths of spirits acting!
> Resound in heart's center
> Human-soul-weaving
> The "I live":
> Thus you stride in earth's course
> As humanity's creative force.

Welten-Sonnen-Kreise,
Geister-Wirkens-Wege!
Tönt in Herzensmitte
Menschen-Seelen-Weben
Das "Ich lebe":
So schreitet Ihr im Erdewandel
Als Menschen-Schöpferkraft.

What I sensed – the moving, the temple dome which arches above, the temple walls. It is all becoming clear for the soul's senses, making the normal world invisible, the world of visible trees, clouds, everything which before was visible. A new visibility appears. The temple, which I only sensed at first, becomes real in the second verse.

And I hear the murmuring, the hissing and rumbling from below:

Cosmic-foundation-powers,
Creator's luster of love!
Create in the body's limbs
Human-action-streams
The "I will":
Thus do you strive in earthly works
as human sensory deeds.

Welten-Grundes-Mächte,
Schöpfer-Liebes-Glänzen!
Schafft in Leibesgliedern
Menschen-Wirkens-Strömung
Das "Ich will":
So strebt Ihr im Erdenwerke
Als Menschen-Sinnes-Taten.

The temple is complete. It has acquired its foundation. And in it are those spiritual beings with whom we as wish to be in communion. The temple is there, visible to the soul's senses. It has been found.

Our meditation does not contain visions. It leads us into the spiritual world. The spiritual world exists. I am describing, my dear sisters and brothers, how the meditation can proceed: the moving temple dome is sensed after the first verse; see the temple around us with the soul's senses. The temple is complete, and the beings with whom we wish to be in communion as humanity's teachers – the godly teachers – are there. We are within the temple, accomplished by the first, second and third verses of a true mantric meditation.

When we become aware that we are finding the temple, then we correctly understand what the content of this esoteric school is meant to be.

LESSON TWELVE

Dornach, May 11, 1924

My dear friends,

First let us recite the verse which reminds us of what comes from the cosmos itself as an invitation to knowledge:

> O man, know thyself!
> So resounds the cosmic-word.
> You hear it strong in soul,
> You feel it firm in spirit.
>
> Who speaks with such cosmic might?
> Who speaks with such depth of heart?
>
> Does it work through distant radiant space
> Into your senses' sense of being?
> Does it ring through waves of time
> Into your life's evolving stream?
>
> Is it you yourself who
> In feeling space, in experiencing time
>
> The Word create, feeling foreign
> In the soulless void of space,
> Because you lose the force of thought
> In time's destructive flow.

Self-knowledge, my dear sisters and brothers, is what, in a spiritual sense, can lead to cosmic knowledge. And it has often been said that understanding must exist for true spiritual cosmic knowledge to stream out of the spiritual world itself; that we must understand that the person who is able to transmit such knowledge from the spiritual world must approach the threshold; that the Guardian of the Threshold stands at the threshold, the Guardian who protects the person in normal consciousness from entering the spiritual world unprepared.

But it is just when one gets to know this Guardian — at first by means of healthy human understanding — then later in its true form, in its real essence, then the Guardian makes known to us the admonishments if we wish to enter the spiritual world in the right way, and then to stand within the experiences of the spiritual world.

It has also often been said that this living in the spiritual world is mostly mistakenly imagined, because one wants something different than really standing within the spiritual world. One wants something which is similar to the sense perceptible world. It is super-sensible though, and can therefore not lead to envisioning something similar to what is seen through the senses. This imaginative-super-sensible envisioning is only an image. It must lead to a real experience of the spiritual world. And many of you, my dear sisters and brothers, have this experience of the spiritual more so than you think. You are only not aware of it. You do not pay attention to how the spirit acts and weaves within psychic experience. It works and weaves. And it is a matter of mustering the intimate mindfulness necessary for perceiving this working and weaving.

Therefore more and more real indications should be given to enable you to feel how the human soul lives in the spiritual world – for knowledge is meant to flow to you directly from the spiritual world through these class lessons, my sisters and brothers. And the following can be such an indication.

Take any of the mantras or other verses and recite it. It doesn't matter much which one it is, it can be any mantra you are familiar with. For your meditation select any mantra and recite it in the fairest way you can. Do it therefor not loudly, but in a soft, gentle manner:

> O man, know thyself!
> So resounds the cosmic-word.
> You hear it strong in soul,
> You feel it firm in spirit.

And then, once you have recited such a mantra to yourself, try to sense how the reciting reacts within you. Try to come to the point where you can sense the speaking, that you sense the difference in your bodies between when you are silent and when you are speaking. Try to sense the speaking in your organism, how it passes through. You will sense it as all kinds of pressure and wave currents in the speech organs.

And when you have sensed this, ask yourselves: When I think something, due to someone talking to me or some other event that makes an impression on me relative to the present: Can I also sense that?

Well, if you have learned to sense speaking, then you will easily be able to sense the thinking which is directly induced by the immediate present. It is lighter and more delicate to sense than speaking, but it can be sensed. And you can learn to sense, to feel thinking by sensing speech.

Then, just as you can sense speech, you can also sense thinking. Then you will be able to touch, touch internally that is, perceive internally, thus: [draws: white outline of a profile]. When speaking is sensed so that it must be moved here [red], you will sense thinking here above [green]. That is, the sense of thinking is moved somewhat up against the back of the head.

Blackboard Drawing for Lesson Twelve

It is good to practice such an exercise, for it acts as a guide to intimate self-observation.

And now you proceed, my dear sisters and brothers, to make a thought active, a remembrance-thought, one which you had days, weeks or months ago and which you can activate just as well now, and try to sense, to feel such a remembrance-thought. And you will have the sensation: I feel this under the region of speech, I feel it here below, under the region of speech [yellow]. And you will then say to yourselves: When I speak, I experience it in the region of my speech organs; when I think, I experience it above in the head, when I remember, I experience it under the region of speech.

When this becomes an intimate experience for you, when you really feel it, then you have grasped something spiritual, which can be the beginning of a progressively increasing spiritual understanding. But a substantial seclusion from the outer events of the day is necessary in order to sense this. It is not good to say: Yes, but in order to achieve such seclusion I'll have to take a few weeks off and go to where there are no people, where nothing can bother me, where I will have absolute peace and quiet, for example in a hut on Mont Blanc. It is not good to think like that, because you will never progress that way. It is better to stand within the tumult of life, exposed to what life brings from morning to night and nevertheless dedicate by strength of soul a period of time, be it ever so short, when you are completely outside of the world's tumult, but at the same time within it, purely by means of your inner force. That is best. To withdraw in solitude in order to have peace is not what works best, but rather to create solitude through one's own forces. That is what definitely and securely can lead to the goal. This is a good foundation for meditating in the right way.

You have learned mantras, my dear sisters and brothers, which are spoken quietly from the soul. The first mantras in these lessons were like that. We have however advanced to mantras which partly ring out to us from the soul and also partly must be imagined as resounding to us from out of the distant universe; where we therefor do not inwardly meditate speaking, but where we inwardly meditate hearing. We imagine ourselves as being transferred to where we hear what is being spoken to us whether it is by the cosmos or by the spirit-beings. And it is just this transferring to a condition in which other beings speak to us that creates the condition which is conducive to feeling that we are in the spiritual world.

Today's mantras will be given with this objective. The mind, the soul should imagine itself as being perfectly silent. But the soul should also imagine itself to already be on the other side of the threshold standing before the Guardian in the spiritual world. And, although being perfectly silent itself, it hears three sounds. The first sound comes from the distant universe; the second from the Guardian. And the third comes from the beings who will be identified later in the mantra. That is how the mantra which is presented to your souls today is to be understood.

Thus, coming from all sides of the distant universe:

Listen to the field of thinking.

It is a question of becoming enlightened concerning the true nature of thinking through a spiritually cosmic experience.

Then the Guardian speaks. After the resounding to us from the distant universe – we must experience this situation spiritually – the Guardian speaks the next three lines:

The one who wants to show to you
The paths from life on earth to life
On earth in spirit light does speak.

That is the Guardian speaking.

Then the angel who shows us the path from earthly life to earthly life speaks:

Behold your senses' shining radiance.

This is the being who as an angel-being, as Angelos, guides us from incarnation to incarnation. It speaks of these goals. We hear them in inner contemplation.

Again the Guardian speaks:
The one who wants to carry you,
Your soul conveyed to souls

in regions matter-free, speaks.

And the next lines are spoken by the being who watches over us from the hierarchy of Archangels:

Behold the forces working in your thinking.

That goes above, to where the Archangels are.

First we had "Behold your senses' shining radiance." This means that for the senses the sun shines and the senses do not; in reality, though, our senses also shine, except that while our senses are shining we are not aware of it. So the being who belongs to us from the ranks of angels admonishes us: "Behold your senses' shining radiance."

In general we think in normal consciousness; but we do not apprehend thinking; we do not sense it, we do not feel it. The being who belongs to us from the ranks of the archangels admonishes us: "Behold the forces working in your thinking."

Now we ascend to where the Archai are. The Guardian advises us that we should listen to the admonishment of the being from the ranks of the Archai. The next three lines are those of the Guardian:

The one speaks who among spirits
in earth-distant fields of creation
Desires to give you the ground of being.

I could also say the "throne of being", but "ground of being" is better, for it is what is to be given to you by the one who wants a spiritual ground in the spiritual field for you, just as here in the sensory field you are standing on physical ground.

After the Guardian of the Threshold has thus spoken, the being from the ranks of the Archai speaks:

Behold the imagery of remembrance.

That is third. First we should see the radiance of the senses, then the forces of thinking working in us, then what lies deep down, below speech, in the memory images: "Behold" the imagery of remembrance.

Thus have we listened with quiet souls to the threefold voice speaking to us: speaking from the cosmos in the very first lines: "Listen to the field of thinking". Then to the intervening three lines by the Guardian of the Threshold, and then to the beings who belong to us from the ranks of the hierarchies, always using paradigmatic lines which are meant to speak to the deepest levels of our being. Together it is like this:

Listen to the field of thinking:

The one who wants to show to you
The paths from life on earth to life
On earth in spirit light does speak.
Behold your senses' shining radiance.

The one who wants to carry you,
Your soul conveyed to souls
in regions matter-free, speaks.
Behold the forces working in your thinking.

The one speaks who among spirits
in earth-distant fields of creation
Desires to give you the ground of being.
Behold the imagery of remembrance.

The first mantra is written on the blackboard. The word "thinking" in the first line is underlined as well as the last lines of 1,2,3.

I. Listen to the field of <u>thinking</u>:

1.) The one who wants to show to you
The paths from life on earth to life
On earth in spirit light does speak.
<u>Behold your senses' shining radiance.</u>

2.) The one who wants to carry you,
Your soul conveyed to souls
in regions matter-free, speaks.
<u>Behold the forces working in your thinking</u>.

3.) The one speaks who among spirits
in earth-distant fields of creation
Desires to give you the ground of being.
Behold the imagery of remembrance.

Therewith we have inwardly experienced the admonishments resounding from the three lower hierarchies for our self-knowledge:

the first from the hierarchy of the   *Angeloi*

the second from the hierarchy of the   *Archangeloi*

the third from the hierarchy of the   *Archai.*

["Angeloi" is written beside part 1, "Archangeloi" beside part 2, "Archai" beside part 3.]

Before the exercise begins, concentration in the soul [mind] can be achieved by imagining a definite image, this image [drawing begins on the image above]: an eye looking upward [eye] and perceiving the higher hierarchies [arc], from which the cosmic forces stream into the eye [upper rays], which then perceives the circle of the lower hierarchies [wavy line], which reach up to the higher hierarchies and send the rays on the human beings [lower rays].

We call this image to mind and hold it there: the eye looking upward, the two lines – the circular one, the wavy one – the descending rays. And while doing the exercise, without thinking about it, the image remains before our soul: the image of the upward looking eye.

Then we hear again, resounding from all sides of the cosmos:
Perceive the field of feeling.
The Guardian then speaks the next three lines:

The one who speaks as thought
From the sun-rays of the spirit
Recalls you to cosmic existence.

It is now a higher language, the language that resounds from higher hierarchies. Whereas there [indicates the first mantra] we are made more attentive to what is already within us, in this mantra we are spoken to by the Guardian in a manner which does not only call us to observe our senses, our thinking and our memories, but we are now meant to hear how we are being called into cosmic being itself. This resounds from the hierarchy of the Exusiai.

Then the one who belongs to us from the hierarchy of the Exusiai speaks:

Feel in your breath life awakening.

Again the Guardian speaks the next three lines:

The one speaks who gives to you
From the stars' living forces
Cosmic being in spirit kingdoms.

Then the being from the hierarchy of the Dynamis speaks:
Feel in your blood's weaving waves.

We must feel the world's weaving movement continued in the weaving waves of our blood.

And the Guardian speaks once more, now advising us that we should listen to what the being from the rank of Kyriotetes says:

The one speaks who wants to create

In the light of the divine heights
The sense of spirit from earthly will.

Then this being from the ranks of the Kyriotetes speaks:
Feel the earth's mighty resistance.

For only if we feel this mighty resistance of the earth's forces can we enter correctly into the world of pure spirit.

Therefore the experience of this mantra must be felt:

Perceive the field of feeling:

The one who speaks as thought
from the sun-rays of the spirit
calls you to cosmic existence:
Feel in your breath life awakening.

The one speaks who gives to you
From the stars' living forces
Cosmic being in spirit kingdoms:
Feel in your blood's weaving waves.

The one speaks who wants to create
In the light of the divine heights
The sense of spirit from earthly will.
Feel the earth's mighty resistance.

It is the ascent to the rank of the second hierarchy where self-knowledge asserts itself in us, where the Guardian advises us that a being from the ranks of the Exusiai will speak to us.

My dear sisters and brothers, we think in earthly life; our thoughts are almost nothing. But when a being from the ranks of the Exusiai thinks, he is thinking us. Our I is being thought. And it, our I, exists as a thought by a being from the ranks of the Exusiai. When on earth we speak "I" to ourselves, where are we looking? Yes, this I: when we say "I" [drawing: circle with the word "Ich", yellow], we are looking back at this *Ich* [red arrows], and say the word "I" [Ich]. But for a being from the ranks of the Exusiai [green line] this I-thought is a real thought. We exist in that we are thought by beings from the ranks of the Exusiai. And when we say "I" to ourselves we are confirming that we are being thought by divine beings. And it is in this being thought by divine beings that our higher being consists.

Then: A being from the ranks of the Dynamis reminds us that the spiritual existence we receive from him as a gift comes from the life-forces taken from the stars.

And a being from the ranks of the Kyriotetes reminds us that what exists in us on earth as will is taken out to the heavenly heights and after the transformation which it undergoes there it is returned to us so that we can then also use it as spirit-will. Earthly will is only a transformation of spirit-will. Earthly will is constantly being taken up and brought down again. Above it is heavenly will; below it is earthly will. Finally the Guardian reminds us that a being from the ranks of the Kyriotetes is saying: "Feel the earth's mighty resistance." When we feel the earth's resistance, we feel the benefit, the grace inherent in the bestowing of forces from the heavenly heights.

[Mantra II is written on the blackboard. In the first line "feeling" is underlined, and the last lines of Parts 1,2 and 3 are also underlined.]

II.) Perceive the field of <u>feeling</u>:

1.) The one who speaks as thought
from the sun-rays of the spirit
calls you to cosmic existence:
<u>Feel in your breath life awakening</u>.

2.) The one speaks who gives to you
From the stars' living forces
Cosmic being in spirit kingdoms:
<u>Feel in your blood's weaving waves</u>.

3.) The one speaks who wants to create
In the light of the divine heights
The sense of spirit from earthly will.
<u>Feel the earth's mighty resistance</u>.

This, then, is the second mantra (recites it):

Perceive the field of feeling:

The one who speaks as thought
from the sun-rays of the spirit
calls you to cosmic existence:
Feel in your breath life awakening.

The one speaks who gives to you
From the stars' living forces
Cosmic being in spirit kingdoms:
Feel in your blood's weaving waves.

The one speaks who wants to create
In the light of the divine heights

The sense of spirit from earthly will.
Feel the earth's mighty resistance.

The first resounds from the ranks of the	Exusiai
The second from the ranks of the	Dynamis
The third from the ranks of the	Kyriotetes

[Exusiai is written alongside part1; Dynamis alongside part 2, Kyriotetes alongside part 3.]

And finally, in order to remember the image we have placed before us after all this has taken place within us, and in order to have a clear experience of it, we recall the image – although we realize that it has been before us during the whole exercise – but we want to place it once more before our souls.

[In the image already drawn on the blackboard, the eye, arc, upper rays, wavy lines, lower rays are drawn again.]

The ascent to the ranks of the Seraphim, Cherubim and Thrones will be added to these in the next class lesson. But now it is appropriate to clarify the meaning of the whole.

My dear sisters and brothers, at the beginning of today's lesson the words from cosmic-being instructed us to practice self-knowledge. Self-knowledge, it was said, leads to world-knowledge; but only if the Self can be in connection with the world.

But the Self does not exist in relation to an external natural entity or process, but alone in relation to the spiritual world. That is where the beings of the hierarchies are. So if we really wish to penetrate into our Self, into our I, then we must experience it together with the beings from the hierarchies and not with external nature. For what we can call our I in external nature is only the distant echo of the I. The true I exists in the same realms as these beings of the higher hierarchies. Therefore in entering the realm of self-knowledge we must also enter the realm of the higher hierarchies. Then we must hear the speech of the higher hierarchies.

The admonishments of the Guardian of the threshold always intervene in order that we do this with all our strength, that we do not make it into a mere bloodless theory. In order that the whole content in the meditation appear before us in all its majesty, we hear the two – and as we will soon hear, three – forceful admonishments from the cosmos: "Behold the field of thinking", "Behold the field of feeling".

Only if we feel the language in such a living, threefold way, and if we experience ourselves within the spiritual world as described in the mantras, then these things will be able to help us advance. For only then will we feel them with the right attitude. We must seek this mental attitude above all. For inner consecration must be there if the meditation is to contribute to initiation. And this inner consecration comes only from the attitude through which we are displaced from the outer world for a while and live exclusively within the content and elements of the meditation. If we can do this so that self-knowledge is not merely an inner brooding, but is an explicit conversation with the world, the Guardian and the Hierarchies, then we will find ourselves in possession of true self-knowledge.

Basically, we should even avoid thinking about such things if we cannot simultaneously evoke the appropriate mental attitude. We should only think about what has been presented today if we can really evoke this inner attitude in the soul, which consists in simply feeling that the sublime majesty from the universe, from the cosmic distances, comes to us like cosmic thunder; that a softly admonishing voice intervenes which comes from the Guardian of the Threshold; and that then one of the beings of the Hierarchies urgently speaks.

Only when we remember this and when we evoke the feeling related to this remembering, should we even think of these mantras or create an inner connection with them, so that we do not desecrate them inwardly, desecrate their force – that we do not think of them with the usual, dry, common way of thinking, which we would think if we did not first evoke the appropriate attitude.

And we therefore should achieve the inner mental attitude to feel that human self-knowledge is something solemn, earnest and holy and that these things should only be spoken internally by the soul – let alone externally – when they are felt to be earnest, solemn, consecrated.

It is a great hindrance to progress on the esoteric path that so much is spoken about these things in a cliquish manner, even with a whiff of vanity and gossip, when this earnest, solemn attitude of consecration has not been developed. We don't realize then that in esoteric life everything depends on the pure, absolute truth prevailing. Whoever does not recognize this – that in esoteric life truth, absolute truth must prevail – can do nothing in esoteric life; that one cannot merely speak of the truth and then regard things as one does as usual in profane life. That happens when we make these things the object of idle gossip.

And this idle gossip which is so much practiced is what throws so many hindrances and obstructions on the esoteric path. And we must necessarily bring together everything related to self-knowledge with an earnest, solemn consecrated attitude. Then we will have allowed the words to correctly work on our souls which were spoken at the beginning of the Class lesson and will be repeated now at the end:

O man, know thyself!

Yes, that is a guide to self-knowledge:

O man, know thyself!
So resounds the cosmic-word.
You hear it strong in soul,
You feel it firm in spirit.

Who speaks with such cosmic might?
Who speaks with such depth of heart?

Does it work through distant radiant space
Into your senses' sense of being?
Does it ring through waves of time
Into your life's evolving stream?

Is it you yourself who
In feeling space, in experiencing time

The Word create, feeling foreign
In the soulless void of space,
Because you lose the force of thought
In time's destructive flow.

Essentially it is a question. The answer is found in the mantras given today.

O Mensch, erkenne dich selbst!
So tönt das Weltenwort.
Du hörst es seelenkräftig,
Du fühlst es geistgewaltig.

Wer spricht so weltenmächtig?
Wer spricht so herzinniglich?

Wirkt es durch des Raumes Weitensgtrahlung
In deines Sinnes Seinserleben?
Tönt es durch der Zeiten Wellenweben?

Bist du es selbst, der sich
Im Raumesfühlen, im Zeiterleben

Das Wort erschafft, dich fremd
Erfühlend in Raumes Seelenleere,
Weil du des Denkens Kraft
Verlierst im Zeitvernichtunsstrom.

LESSON THIRTEEN

Dornach, May 17, 1924

My dear Friends,

First of all we shall speak the imperative words from the spirit of the cosmos which urge us to self-observation for knowledge of our being:

> O man, know thyself!
> So sounds the Cosmic-Word.
> You hear it strong in soul,
> You feel it firm in spirit.
>
> Who speaks with such cosmic might?
> Who speaks with such depth of heart?
>
> Does it work through distant radiant space
> Into your senses' sense of being?
> Does it ring through weaving waves of time
> Into your life's evolving stream?
>
> It's you yourself who,
> In feeling space, in experiencing time
>
> The Word create, feeling foreign
> In the soulless void of space,
> Because you lose the force of thought
> In time's destructive flow.

My dear sisters and brothers, in the previous lesson we tried to find the inner psychic words which can bring our humanity into contact with what is revealed by the spiritual hierarchies – with which the human spirit is closely related. We placed before our souls how by concentrating on the field of thinking we could rise up to the region where the beings of the third hierarchy reside, so to speak: the Angels, Archangels and Archai.

Not meant is our everyday thinking, but the thinking which acts behind that everyday thinking, which we can only achieve from our whole being by meditating deeply on the words which begin with: "Perceive the field of thinking."

And I also pointed out last time how this thinking can be perceived in the human organism itself *above* the region of speech; whereas the field of memory-thought can be felt *under* the region of speech. In respect to the region of speech itself: when we say something innerly and intensely in a low voice, or even out loud, we feel the speaking within and we can designate the place where we feel the speaking within us. Then we have a starting point, for it is more or less easy to experience this speech.

And over the speaking, more toward the rear of the head, we can find the inner thinking through which we can discover the Angeloi; in the speaking itself the Archangeloi; and in remembrance, under the speaking, the Archai can be felt.

And the mantric verse which leads us to this point was described in the previous class lesson.

By means of this verse we imagine how at first cosmic space speaks, the universe itself resounds to us, so to speak, and therewith the Guardian of the Threshold tells us to be attentive to what the beings related to us from the ranks of the third hierarchy, the Angeloi, have to say.

Then, secondly, how the Guardian of the Threshold again admonishes us to be attentive to the beings related to us from the ranks of the Archangeloi.

And thirdly, the Guardian again admonishes us to listen attentively to the beings related to us from the ranks of the Archai. So we should imagine this mantric verse so that we hear the universe from the distant cosmos resounding to us, and hear the Guardian and the hierarchies speaking:

Perceive the field of thinking:

The one who wants to show to you

The paths from life on earth to life

On earth in spirit light does speak.

Behold your senses' shining radiance.

The one who wants to carry you,

Your soul conveyed to souls

In regions matter-free, speaks.

Behold the forces working in your thinking.

The one speaks who among spirits

In earth-distant fields of creation

Desires to give you the ground of being.

Behold the imagery of remembrance.

So if we can always feel ourselves in this situation – the cosmic distances speaking to us, the Guardian of the Threshold speaking to us, the ranks of the hierarchies speaking to us, if we can vividly imagine it as though it were around us, then in relation to the schematic picture I drew on the blackboard the last time, we gradually come to sense the thinking above the place of speech in the back of the head, through which we approach the movement and the life of the third hierarchy.

And so, my dear sisters and brothers, we can say that by means of this mantric verse we come in contact with the beings of the third hierarchy.

Likewise do we come into contact with the beings of the second hierarchy through the second mantric verse, which was also set forth and which should also be felt and spiritually perceived, so to speak. We should ignore the fact that we are saying it; we should transpose ourselves into the situation I described.

Perceive the field of feeling:

The one who speaks as thought

From the sun-rays of the spirit

Calls you to cosmic existence:

Feel in your breath life awakening.

The one speaks who gives to you

From the stars' living forces

Cosmic being in spirit kingdoms:

Feel in your blood's weaving waves.

The one speaks who wants to create

In the light of the divine heights

The sense of spirit from earthly will.

Feel the earth's mighty resistance.

Thus we come into contact with the Exusiai, Dynamis, Kyriotetes, An inner connection is created between the feeling sphere – breathing and blood circulation – and where the will arises, but which is only *felt* as will – and through which a connection is created between everything in our humanity and the beings of the second hierarchy.

What remains for us to consider today, my dear sisters and brothers, is the field of volition, of will. The field of the will is the one which most dominates the human being, which acts most strongly in him, but is also the one which is least experienced with real attention. For man usually knows little of how the will acts.

Let us take first where the will is most evident in the human organism, that is, when the human organism is set in motion.

You must, my dear sisters and brothers, adopt these intimate concepts if you want to penetrate into what the spirit which speaks through this esoteric school wishes to indicate as the path.

Imagine yourself walking, and perhaps moving your arms. Normally we think that we moves our legs and the legs carry us forward. This is the most convenient idea one can have. We thinks that an unknown force – it is of course an unknown force, for nobody with normal consciousness can know anything about this force – streams into the legs. Each leg is placed before the other. Thus we carry ourselves through the world.

But such is not the case. In no way do the legs have the primary task of carrying us through the world. It is simply not true. Here we come to a subject where normal consciousness immediately shows its maya; for it is maya when we believe that we walk with the legs, with the physical legs, that the physical legs exist for walking.

Of course this does not mean, my dear sisters and brothers, that you should go out into the world of triviality and cry out-loud: "It is not true that man has his legs in order to walk." For that would of course not be understood at first. Because the profound sense in which it is true is unknown – that almost everything normal consciousness offers us at first is maya, the great illusion. The great illusion does not only include what we observe around us, but also how we experience ourselves in the world.

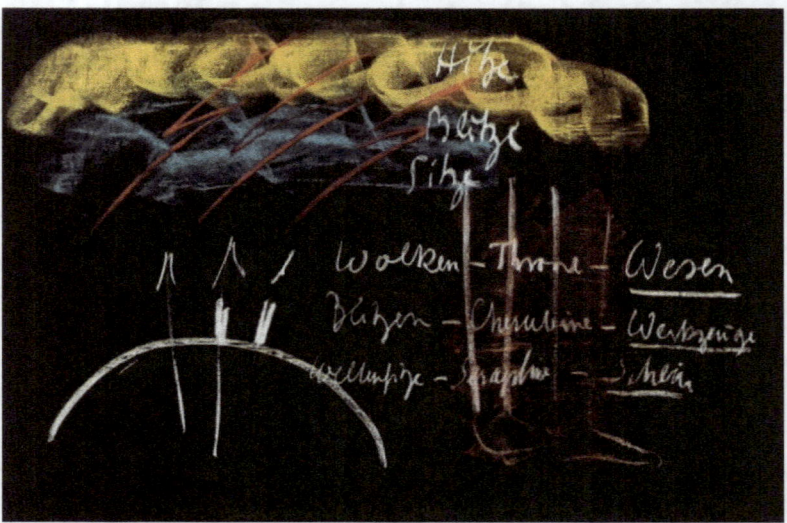

Blackboard Drawing from Lesson Thirteen

Imagine the following [drawing]: these are human legs – where each one strides before the other [white legs]. But within these physical human legs is the human etheric body [red]; the part of the human etheric body that corresponds to the legs; here is the astral body [yellow] the part which corresponds to the legs, and then the I-organization [violet]. We don't walk with the physical legs, we don't walk with the etheric legs, not even with the astral legs, but we walk with the forces that correspond to the I-organization. We live with these forces, which correspond to the I-organization, in the gravitational forces of the earth, which are of course invisible. [drawing: arc with arrows]. These gravitational forces of the earth we experience with our I-organization forces [short strokes on the arrows] – and the will which governs movement – which acts between the invisible I-organization and the invisible gravitational forces of the earth.

Now the I-organization is so constituted that it needs to feel something like resistance when it comes into contact with the earth's gravitational forces. The legs' astral body serves this purpose, also the etheric body and, especially, the physical body, in order that the I-organization can feel itself, can perceive itself. And without this perception it could not have a connection with the earth-organization – because it must be conscious of this connection. In order that in walking the I-organization may be conscious of itself and come into contact with the earth-organization, the physical and the other organizations are present.

Therefor walking is a super-sensible process. The sensible organization is only present in order that the walking be perceived, because it can be accomplished only when it is perceived. You no more walk with your legs, my dear sisters and brothers, than you do with your stockings. You walk with what corresponds to your I-organization in your legs. And just as you have stockings to provide warmth, so do you have physical legs in order to provide consciousness for walking.

What I have just said must be felt. We must learn to feel when walking that walking is a super-sensible process, and that the sensible is only there in order to provide consciousness of the process. During waking earth-life this consciousness is created in a less than perfect way, because our legs are also heavy, so we not only come into contact with the gravitational pull of the earth, but also with the gravitational force that acts in our legs. Therefor when we are not using our physical legs, as in sleep, we speed around the universe in the I and astral body in a much more agile way than when we move about in physical life. We do move about during sleep, only we have no consciousness of doing so, because the physical legs provide that consciousness.

Who is it then who provides us with the capacity for movement during sleep – and then also during clairvoyance? We are able to move, I said, in physical life because the movement becomes conscious through the physical legs. Who, my dear friends, does that instead when we are sleeping? Those beings who connect with us for the purpose of movement when we are sleeping. They are the Thrones, beings of the First Hierarchy. However, with normal consciousness, with normal sleeping consciousness, man cannot perceive the Thrones; therefor it doesn't help. But when through intuition he is capable of perceiving what happens during sleep, he becomes aware that during sleep he is in contact with a higher world through the Thrones, just as in physical life he is in contact with normal earth life through his physical legs.

All this we must translate into feeling. We must learn to sense it. And then we will sense the interweaving, undulating spiritual world in which we always are.

And we can again rise to such an inner feeling and experience if we let it work upon us in this situation as we did in respect to the other mantras which I described for the field of thinking and the field of feeling: from out of the cosmos comes an urgent voice like thunder, then the Guardian of the Threshold tells us to listen to the Thrones speaking to us. The Thrones speak to us about the drives – as they are called – the instinctual drives which are transferred to our volition when we carry out an act of will.

Therefore, we will let the third part of this mantra work on us, as it resounds again from the cosmos:

Perceive the field of will

Then the Guardian of the threshold:

The one who guides the cosmic forces
From the dull dark earth-foundations
Into your limbs' movements, speaks:
Behold your fiery instinctual drives.

That is the first. The second leads us more into the soul [psychological] aspect. If we continue to investigate the human will's actions in this deep meditative practice we make a great discovery. And at some point humanity must make this discovery if it wishes to advance in the field of evolution.

Now I must indicate something to you, my dear sisters and brothers, something you all know, for normal consciousness is already aware of it. It is what we call the voice of conscience in us. The voice of conscience! But the voice of conscience calls out in an indeterminate way to human consciousness. Usually we do not rightly know what it is – in respect to our moral-psychological comportment – that comes from the mysterious depths of our souls and which we call the voice of conscience. With normal consciousness one does not penetrate so deeply into one's own being as to reach the voice of conscience. It ascends, but man does not reach it, so he does not look at it face to face.

And when man penetrates meditatively to the distant world of the Cherubim, the wisdom filled beings who live and act throughout the universe, he makes the great discovery that from the world of the cherubim an impulse enters into him within which the voice of conscience lives. Oh, the voice of conscience is of high origin, high being. It actually lives in the world of the Cherubim. From that world of the Cherubim it weaves itself into humanity and at first resounds from the depths of this humanity in an indeterminate way. But it is a great, mighty encounter when man, through intuition, can come into contact with the field of the Cherubim and encounter the world where his conscience lives and works. It is the greatest personal discovery anyone can make.

Therefor the Guardian of the Threshold admonishes us with the following words:

The one speaks who with grace

Lets the clear spirit-rays from God's

Fields of action, circulate in your blood:

Behold the soul-guide of your conscience.

In truth it is the spirit from the field of the Cherubim that circulates in the blood that constitutes the voice of conscience. The blood is physical in all the parts of our bodies; but in that it is physical in all the parts of our bodies, it carries the voice of conscience, along with other things. And the waves of Cherubim life interweave in our blood.

We will gain an important place for this meditation if we imagine the situation thus:

First speaks what originates in the universal distance:

Behold the field of will.

The Guardian of the Threshold admonishes us:

The one who guides the cosmic forces

From the dull dark earth-foundations

Into your limbs' movements, speaks:

Then we imagine [drawing] interweaving clouds [blue] symbolizing the Thrones. And in that we imagine these interweaving clouds, we hear the Thrones, the voices from the first hierarchy:

Behold your fiery instinctual drives.

Then the Guardian of the Threshold continues:

The one speaks who with grace

Lets the clear spirit-rays from God's

Fields of action, circulate in your blood.

Now we imagine lightning [red] flashing through the clouds, for lightning is the tool of the Cherubim, the fiery swords of the Cherubim. As the lightning flashes through the clouds, we feel these flashes in the words:

Behold conscience's soul-guidance.

Then the Guardian of the Threshold speaks:
The one speaks who brings the accomplished in man, that is, in the previous earth lives:

Sensibly through death and birth,

To breathe again in contemporary times.

Now we imagine the entire sky above the lightning with weaving warmth [drawing: yellow], sending the lightning down with heat. And in this weaving heat from the cosmos we sense the Seraphim's speech:

Behold your destiny's spiritual trial -

how destiny extends from earth-life to earth-life to the present earth-life.

This mantra is especially effective when it is felt combined in this way with the image. And we can prepare ourselves for this mantra by using the good German word "Sitze" – after denuding it of all triviality – instead of Thrones say "Sitze" (seats).

So imagine, my dear sisters and brothers, that you feel the word "Sitze",

[it is written on the blackboard:]   *Sitze (seats)*

Flashes in the clouds; form the idea of clouds in your minds – the word *"Blitze"* (lightning bolts)

["Blitze" is written over "Sitze"]   *Blitze (lightning bolts)*

again with the idea of "flashing through": the lightning flashing in the clouds. You form the word "Hitze".

["Hitze" is written over "Blitze"]   *Hitze (heat)*

Universal heat; and feel in this threefold "i" [pronounced "ee"] the ascending from the cloud flashes to the lightning bolts and to the universal heat, from which the lightning bolts derive. You feel prepared for the mantra:

Sitze, Blitze, Hitze.

And then, after this scene is before you, feel with the image the force of the mantra:

[Mantra III is written on the blackboard. The word "will" and the last lines of all three parts are underlined.]

III. Behold the field of will.

1.) The one who guides the cosmic forces
from the dull dark earth-foundations
into your limbs' movements, speaks:
Behold your fiery instinctual drives.

2.) The one speaks who with grace
lets the clear spirit-rays from God's
fields of action, circulate in your blood.
Behold conscience's soul-guidance.

3.) The one speaks who brings the accomplished in man
sensibly through death and birth,

to breathe again in contemporary times.

<u>*Behold your destiny's spiritual trial.*</u>

Nothing in such verses is mere empty phrase: rather is it about the limbs' active movement. I described it as a working together of the I-organization with the forces of the earth – a super-sensible process. We must be aware of that in the first part of the mantra.

In the second part of the mantra we must be aware of the blood circulating throughout the whole organism, containing everything pertaining to the conscience. However, our destiny basically lives in our breathing – the uppermost part of our rhythmic system – insofar as it is streamed through not only with what today enlivens us in breathing, but because breathing has been formed by earlier stages of earthly existence.

Here [in part 1] the Guardian of the Threshold refers us

to the   *Thrones*

here [in part 2] to the   *Cherubim*

here [in part 3] to the   *Seraphim*

["Thrones" is written beside part 1, "Cherubim" beside part 2, "Seraphim" beside part 3.]

The symbol we choose to give the mantra the necessary strength and spiritual consolidation and which expresses the first Hierarchy's revelation in a beautiful way: clouds , but at the same time what the Thrones derive their substance from – when we observe the spiritual in the clouds: their own being or essence.

[The following is written, with "being" underlined.]

clouds – Thrones – <u>being</u>

We look up to the lightning bolts. Oh, the Cherubim are already more hidden. We can sense how the Thrones are acting and moving in the clouds. The looming clouds provide the Thrones with substance. The Cherubim do not make it easy for us to see them. They are more hidden than the Thrones. They do not show themselves in the formations. They show us their tools in the lightning bolts. They do not show us their being in the lightning bolts, only their tools.

[The following is written on the blackboard, with "tools" underlined.]

Lightning bolts – Cherubim – <u>tools</u>

And if we ascend to the cosmic heat, the Seraphim are hidden deeply therein, much deeper than the Cherubim are hidden behind their tools, the lightning bolts. The heat is only the shining of the Seraphim. The Thrones reveal themselves by their being; the Cherubim reveal themselves by their tools; the Seraphim reveal themselves by their shining.

[The following is written on the blackboard, with "shining" underlined.]

Cosmic heat – Seraphim – <u>shining</u>

Thus we establish the connection between man and the first Hierarchy in the field of will:

Perceive the field of will:

The one who guides the cosmic forces
From the dull dark earth-foundations
Into your limbs' movements, speaks:
Behold your fiery instinctual drives.

The one speaks who with grace
Lets the clear spirit-rays from God's
Fields of action, circulate in your blood.
Behold conscience's soul-guidance.

The one speaks who brings the accomplished in man
Sensibly through death and birth,
To breathe again in contemporary times.
Behold your destiny's spiritual trial.

In this situation, it is necessary that we feel as though we are not ourselves speaking, thinking, feeling and willing; rather that we completely forget ourselves and feel spoken to in a resounding threefold way.

Yes, my dear sisters and brothers, it is certainly necessary that such mantric procedures be taken most seriously. Then they are effective, as they are meant to be. Then they bring us forward, forward on the threefold fields of the spiritual worlds, on the fields of thinking, feeling and willing. And it is always necessary that we be able to undertake them earnestly.

Something else is necessary which must be taken into account. The meditator will often fall back into the humdrum routine of everyday life. He must do so because between birth and death he is an earthly being. He must always return to his normal consciousness. For example when we have some kind of ache which becomes chronic, we will always feel it. We can sometimes overlook it, but we feel that it is there. We can feel something similar when we have been embraced by the power of meditation. We should always be able to say to ourselves: this normal consciousness has meditated. It has been embraced by the prevailing power of meditation. We should feel that the meditation is present, that we were once in it. By feeling that meditation makes us into something different, we should have become a different person. Having once begun, we can never in life forget, not even for a moment, my dear sisters and brothers, that we are meditants. That is the right attitude.

We should live into meditative life in such a way – naturally for short enough intervals that it does not disturb our normal lives – that we always feel ourselves to be meditants, and when there are moments when we forget that we are meditants, then we should feel as ashamed as if we were walking completely naked along a street crowded with people. We should experience the transition from non-meditant to meditant in such a way that if we forget that we are meditants and then realize that we have forgotten, we are ashamed.

And then we will really advance in what is said to us by the cosmic words with which we began:

> O man, know thyself!
> So sounds the cosmic-word.
> You hear it strong in soul,
> You feel it firm in spirit.
>
> Who speaks with such cosmic might?
> Who speaks with such depth of heart?
>
> Does it work through distant radiant space
> Into your senses' sense of being?
> Does it ring through weaving waves of time
> Into your life's evolving stream?

> Is it you yourself who,
> In feeling space, in experiencing time
>
> The Word create, feeling foreign
> In the soulless void of space,
> Because you lose the force of thought
> In time's destructive flow.

But we must always remember that knowledge is a serious thing, and that the world of great illusions, the world of maya, will not deliver it to us, that we must first arrive at the threshold where the Guardian stands, and that on the threshold all the deceptive forms with which normal sense-perception and normal consciousness is full will disappear.

Then we can perceive additional words from the same cosmic depths from which the words just spoken to us came:

> Know first the earnest Guardian,
>
> Who stands before spirit-land's gates,
>
> Denying entry to your sensible forces
>
> And to your understanding's power,
>
> For in your senses' interweaving
>
> And in your thoughts' forming
>
> From space's lack of being,
>
> From time's power of deception
>
> you must first forcefully conquer
>
> Your own being's truth.

When we have heard such words, the answering words can reverently issue from the depths of our souls:

> I entered this world of sense-perception,
>
> Taking with me thinking's heritage,
>
> A god's strength had led me here.
>
> Death stands at the long path's end.

RUDOLF STEINER

I want to feel the being of Christ

Who wakens in death-of-matter spirit-birth.

Thus I find the world in spirit

And know myself in world's becoming.

———————

LESSON FOURTEEN

Dornach, May 31, 1924

My Dear Friends,

We have been considering the human being's relation to the Guardian of the Threshold and have led our souls step by step to see what our relation is to the Guardian of the Threshold on the path of knowledge. Today we intend to enliven the situation of standing before the Guardian in order to advance a step further in this esoteric consideration.

I will repeat what has been considered in the previous lessons regarding this situation. Man leaves the physical world in which he develops his normal consciousness. He realizes that although this sensible-physical world can be wonderful, joyful as well as painful and full of suffering, it can also be majestic – and that he has every reason to consciously be a part of it. But he also realizes that he can never know himself if he merely directs his attention and his feelings to this physical world. He must say to himself: As wonderful as it is, with all its amazing variety of colors and forms, what I myself am, what my origin and being are, cannot be found in the scope of this environment.

Nevertheless, from all sides the words resound as the most important task in the life of the human being: O man, know thyself!

And it also becomes clear that in normal life we are protected from entering unprepared into the world which is the world of his real being. And the Guardian of the Threshold is the one who protects us from consciously perceiving his environment when we are sleeping at night, for what we would then perceive, unprepared, would be such a terrible shock that we would not be able to lead a normal human waking life.

The Guardian of the Threshold also makes it clear to us that he – the Guardian of the Threshold – is the true, the real gateway to the spiritual world.

Thus the person realizes that before he enters the kingdom of knowledge, he comes to an abyss, which at first seems bottomless. The support of the physical world ends here. He cannot cross it. One can only cross this abyss by freeing oneself from the physical, when one – symbolically speaking - "grows wings", in order to cross the abyss as a psychic-spiritual being.

But the Guardian of the Threshold calls forth to him how to beware of the abyss, especially to be aware of the beasts which rise up as spiritual figures from this abyss, that one should realize that these beasts are the outer reflections of impure willing, feeling and thinking – that they first must be overcome. And in a graphic image one sees how his willing, feeling and thinking appear in three animals – one ghastly, one horrid to look at, and so forth.

Then the Guardian of the Threshold shows us how thinking, feeling and willing can strengthen themselves after having consciously determined to overcome the beasts. To enter the spiritual world, to visualize the spiritual world, we need to develop situation-meditations, in order to feel how the cosmos speaks to us, how the hierarchies speak to us, how at first everything foretells what awaits us there in the spiritual world.

And from what has entered our souls through the mantras, we will realize ever more that the human being must become different when he crosses the abyss, when he wishes to live into what is beyond the abyss. We will realize ever more: Here on earth we associate with the beings of the three nature kingdoms and with humans; beyond we associate with disembodied souls and with the spirits of the higher hierarchies. It is a different kind of relating, which requires a different state of mind.

It is again the task of the Guardian of the Threshold to strongly indicate how the human being must comport himself when faced with the fact that when he crosses the abyss and experiences something of the reality of the spiritual world, he must do so with a completely different state of mind.

The person will realize that two states of mind can be a reality within him: the one on this side of the abyss with normal consciousness; and the one beyond the abyss, outside the physical and etheric bodies – the state of mind in the purely spiritual world.

When the difference between these states of mind appears, great dangers await him, dangers which appear at first to be slight deviations from the normal state of mind which are always present within the psyche, but which are pathological deformities when carried to an extreme. Of course it must be emphasized: When the journey to the higher worlds is undertaken as it is carefully described in my book *Knowledge of the Higher Worlds and its Attainment,* in many shorter works which have appeared in anthroposophical circles, and in the second part of my *An Outline of Occult Science,* then aberration from the normal condition of the mind cannot occur, not even in the slightest degree. The person will cross into the spiritual world in the full consciousness of normal human understanding, first in knowledge and also through initiation. But he must know how, in two ways, he may lose the everyday capacity for understanding, which holds him securely to life, if he does not adhere to the right guidelines into the spiritual world.

Here on this side of the threshold we are standing on the earth, on the solid earthly elements. The ground is beneath our feet, it is our support. Around us is the watery element, which also participates in the formation of our own bodies. In ordinary life this watery element cannot support us, but it interpenetrates us, transforms itself into our blood. It is contained in our growth, in our forces of nutrition. We breathe the air. The airy or gaseous element is all around us. Warmth is all around us: the warmth ether, the fourth element.

In ordinary life they are separate from each other. Where there is solid earth there is not water; where there is water there is not air; where there is air there is not water. Only fire – warmth – interpenetrates all. It is the only thing which interpenetrates everything.

The moment we leave the physical body – also with the first push, my dear friends – this separation of the elements ceases. We enlarge ourselves, we expand, and at the same time we are in earth, water, fire, air. We can no longer distinguish them from each other and the individual attributes of these four elements have ceased to exist. The earth is no longer our support, for it is no longer solid. The water no longer forms us, for its formative force has ended. Once in the spiritual world it is as though we were dissolving, as ice melts in warm water, for we have become one with the water. We could not float in it, for that would mean that we were still separate from it. The blood is no longer a separate element in the blood vessels, but our blood becomes one with the all-pervading watery element of the universe. And air: it ceases being the formative breathing force in us. Warmth ceases to enkindle us to an I, and make us feel that we are a Self within the warmth. It all ends. We must meet this ending of the differentiation between earth, water, air and fire in the right frame of mind.

Imagine that we have already flown over the abyss. We have arrived on the other side, my dear sisters and brothers. The Guardian of the Threshold calls out to us, we should turn around again and face him.

Imagine it vividly, my dear sisters and brothers. The person has arrived on the other side, where the truths and knowledge of the spirit will be revealed to him. He stands on the other side. The Guardian of the Threshold invokes him to turn around in order to receive the advice he needs now that he has been touched by the state of mind which is on the other side of the threshold, where one lives within the four elements: in earth, water, air, fire.

He encounters there – pardon the trivial expression, my dear sisters and brothers – the illusion of being in love with release from the solid earth, from the formative water force, from the creative force of air, from the selfhood awakening force of warmth; he feels delight in spiritual beatitude, dedicated to it and wishes to remain in this state of spiritual beatitude. It overcomes him because the Luciferic temptation is approaching him. Depending on his karma, he can be more or less susceptible to this temptation. If he is so susceptible that he is utterly in love with the experience of dissolving into earth, water, air and fire, the Luciferic forces will apprehend him and he will no longer leave this state of mind. He succumbs to the danger of continuing in this state of mind when he returns to everyday life.

The Guardian of the Threshold must call out to him: You may not do that. You may not succumb to Lucifer. You may not merely feel the delight of bliss in dissolving in earth, water, fire, air. When you return to the physical world you must again take on the state of mind of ordinary consciousness; otherwise in the future you will be an unstable person in the physical world.

That is the Luciferic danger, that upon return from the spiritual world, from beyond the threshold, one becomes an unstable, confused person, no longer versed in the ways of the world, a dreamer who confuses dreaming for idealism and who is contemptuous of ordinary consciousness. That you must not do. And the Guardian of the Threshold urgently admonishes us that we must resolve to live in the world, be it the earthly, be it the spiritual, in the way which corresponds to each.

But the Guardian of the Threshold adds a second admonishment: that when we cross over with separated thinking, feeling and willing, we must pay attention to what extent earthly inclinations are still present in this thinking, feeling and willing.

The person may be inclined to fixate on his experiences on this side of the threshold because of having the earth's support, and cross the threshold in a materialistic state of mind, cross with the congealed formative forces of water. If so, he can be plagued by earthly arrogance and say to himself: In life on earth I breathed, inhaled that breath from which the Father-God once created the human soul, human life. I can also do that if only I am freed from earthly limitations.

But if the person wants to bring over into the spiritual world what he has of creative divine force through his breath, he will succumb to the Ahrimanic temptation. Then he will not be able to return, because before he does so he will become faint. He will be more or less unconscious. His consciousness will be paralyzed. Because his consciousness has been paralyzed, he more or less becomes an instrument of the Ahrimanic powers in the spiritual world.

Although today humanity is crudely hardened by materialism, since the beginning of the Michael age it is practically being dragged over into the spiritual world by spiritual life itself. And what it means when the Ahrimanic powers seize humanity when its consciousness is paralyzed, though otherwise in a fully waking state, has been amply demonstrated, my dear friends, by the outbreak of the great [first] World War.

When this World War broke out, I said to many people: The history of this war can not be written from the physical plane alone. Documents alone do not speak the truth, because of the thirty or forty men in Europe who directly participated in the outbreak of the war, many of them had dimmed consciousness at the decisive moments. They became instruments for the ahrimanic powers on this side. So that much of what happened during this war was instigated by the Ahrimanic powers. The war can only be written about in an occult way.

What is seen – in many respects modified on this side of the threshold – in many leading personalities at the outbreak of this World War, can be observed in those who preserved the habits of the mind and carried them over beyond the threshold and whose consciousness became paralyzed, muted, and they became instruments of the Ahrimanic powers.

It must be perfectly clear that the human being may not carry over to this side the state of mind applicable to beyond the threshold, and that he may not carry over to the other side the state of mind applicable to this side. Rather must he develop a strong inner human consciousness for each domain – for this side and for beyond the threshold.

That applies to all four elements in the Guardian of the Threshold's admonition. We shall now work on these admonitions in meditation.

So let us imagine, my dear sisters and brothers, that you are standing on the other side of the threshold. The Guardian beckons. You look at his face. At first he calls out to you, admonishing:

Where is the earth's solidity which supported you?

We no longer have it. But the inner heart is motivated to give an answer. But this heart can be innerly motivated in a threefold way to an answer from the cosmos.

It can be motivated from the Christ and his power. Then it answers:

I abandon its foundation – the earth's solidity, that is – as long as the spirit supports me.

That is the correct attitude, that I abandon the earth's support as long as the spirit carries me in the spirit-domain, as long as I am out of the body. But the heart can also be motivated by Lucifer. Then it answers:

I feel rapture, for from now on I do not need its support.

That is how one speaks with arrogance, with pride, as though he also does not need the support when he returns to the physical world.

Or the heart can be motivated by Ahriman. Then it answers:

I will hammer it down even harder – the support – with the spirit's power, and bring it over with me.

No one should recoil from meditatively calling to mind again and again all three answers in order to freely choose the first one. For he must feel: the inner self tends to waver to Lucifer, and to Ahriman. One must keep this in mind during meditation.

For the earth element the meditation must therefore contain:

[The first part of the mantra is written on the blackboard. (Writing is always shown in italics).]

1) The Guardian – speaks – Where is the earth's solidity, which supported you?

The Human heart must answer. If it is motivated by Christ, it answers:

Christ: I leave its foundation as long as the spirit supports me.

If the soul is motivated by Lucifer, it answers:

Lucifer: I feel rapture, for from now on I do not need its support.

Now the heart omits "<u>as long as</u>" if it wants to replace the temporal with the eternal, which transforms the sentence. If the heart is motivated by Ahriman, it answers:

Ahriman: I will hammer it down even harder – the support – *with the spirit's power.*

In order that the soul fully dedicate itself to what is coming, we have the Guardian of the Threshold's second admonition, which is related to water's formative force. This formative force of water forms the solid organs in us from the liquid elements. All that we consume for nourishment must first become liquid, from which the organs are formed. All our sharply contoured organs are formed out of the liquid element. This formative force terminates once we tread the realm beyond the threshold. The Guardian warns us that this is the case. He calls to us once we stand on the other side of the Threshold facing his stern countenance:

[The second part of the mantra is written on the blackboard.]

Guardian: Where is the water's formative force which pervaded you?

The person answers if he is motivated in his heart by Christ:

My life extinguishes it, as long as the spirit forms me.

Christ: My life extinguishes it ("it" is the formative force), <u>as long as</u> *the spirit forms me.*

Again, in a modest way, "as long as" is used.

Now, when one is over there out of the body, the spirit is beginning to form.

If the soul is motivated by Lucifer, it leaves out "as long as" and forms the sentence in a prideful, arrogant way:

Lucifer: My life melts it away – what is extinguished can be re-kindled; what melts remains melted – *so I am released from it.*

If the soul is motivated by Ahriman, it answers:

Ahriman: My life solidifies it, so I transfer it to the spirit-realm.

Observe, my dear sisters and brothers, how everything in mantric verses is innerly certain and meaningfully formed. Here [in the first verse] is: "I leave", "I feel", "I will". The "I" speaks in the answer. In the second verse the I no longer speaks egocentrically, but it says: "My life": "my life dissolves", "my life melts", "my life solidifies". It is all appropriate to reality if correctly spoken in the spirit. The carelessness in formulating sentences, which is common in the physical realm, may not be brought over into the spirit-realm. In the spirit-realm all that is spoken must be precise and exact.

You must understand, my dear friends, the reality that this Esoteric School is not established by human will, but by the spiritual world, as I said at the beginning. Everything given here in the Esoteric School of the Goetheanum is only spoken through my lips, but is dictated by the spiritual world. It must be that way in every legitimately existing esoteric school – also in the present and in the immediate future, as it was in the ancient holy Mysteries. And this Esoteric School is the true Michael- School, the institution of those spiritual beings who possess the inspiration of Michael's cosmic will.

In respect to air, the Guardian of the Threshold speaks again, warningly: Where is the air's stimulating force which awakened you? – awakened you to existence.

Just as Jehovah formed a feeling being from a merely living being by means of living breath and the stimulating power of air, so can a human being become a feeling being through the stimulation exercised on his senses by the outer world. What, though, are the senses?

My dear sisters and brothers, the senses are nothing other than differentiated breathing organs. Eye, ear – all are refined breathing organs. Breathing expands to all the senses. As it lives in the lung, it lives in the eye. Except that in the lungs it combines with carbon, and in the ears with highly rarefied silica. Carbon dioxide is formed in the organism. [He draws on the blackboard: "Kohlensäure" = carbon dioxide (red)] In the senses, very fine silicic acid is formed ["Kieselsäure" = silicic acid yellow.]

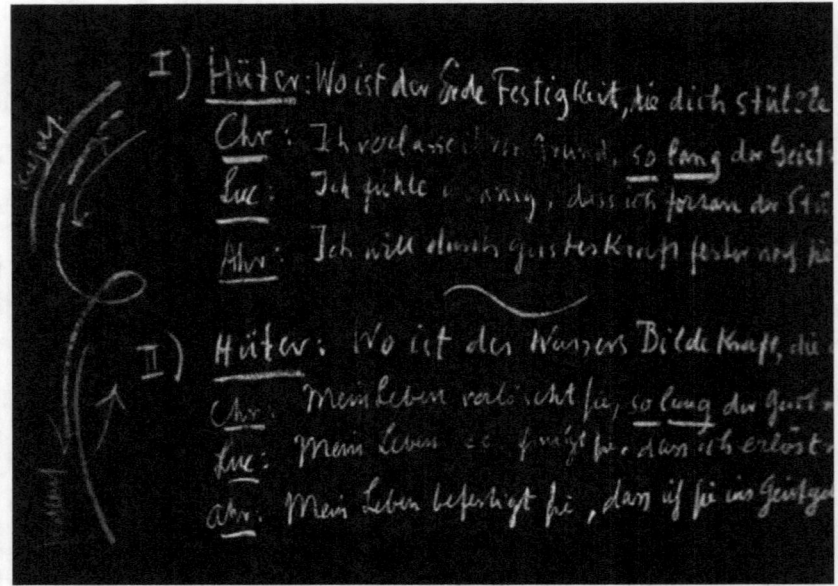

Blackboard Drawing For Lesson Fourteen

Man lives downward by converting oxygen to carbon dioxide. He lives upward into the zone of his sense-nervous For Lesson system by combining oxygen with silica, forming very fine silicic acid. [green]. So we live in a way that when breath turns to blood, it generates carbon dioxide; when breath passes around the senses it generates silicic acid – downward and outward through breath: carbon dioxide; toward the senses and back from the senses to the breathing process in very fine doses of silicic acid.

The Guardian of the Threshold calls to us about all that is in the air:

Where is the air's stimulating force, which awakened you?

He who is motivated in his heart by Christ answers:

My soul breathes the air of heaven – no longer the air of earth, the air of heaven – as long as the spirit surrounds me.

The heart motivated by Lucifer answers:

My soul regards it not in the spirit's rapture.

The heart motivated by Ahriman answers:

My soul absorbs it, that I may learn divine creation.

As Jehovah once created with air, the ahrimanically-minded absorbs the air in order to carry it over to the spiritual world.

The Guardian speaks to the human being:

[The third part of the mantra is written on the blackboard:]

Guardian: Where is the air's stimulating force, which awakened you?

The heart motivated by Christ speaks:

Christ: My soul breathes the air of heaven, as long as the spirit surrounds me.

The heart motivated by Lucifer speaks:

Lucifer: My soul regards it not in the spirit's rapture.

The heart motivated by Ahriman speaks:

Ahriman: My soul absorbs it, that I may learn divine creation.

About fire, the warmth element, the Guardian now speaks the last of his element-words, warning the human not to lose himself in the warmth element as it is experienced in physical earthly existence, but also not to carry it over to the spiritual world.

Beforehand, my dear sisters and brothers, I want to draw your attention to the ascending direction:

"I" the human being says at first.

"My life" the human being says.

"My soul" says the human being.

Now the Guarding speaks warningly about the fire element:

[The fourth part of the mantra is written on the blackboard:]

Guardian: Where is fire's cleansing – or purification – *which ignited your I?*

Our I lives in what pervades us as warmth, as fire. In these esoteric classes, my dear sisters and brothers, I have already indicated once that his solid element remains in man's unconscious, the liquid element also, although one does feels pleasure at being in the liquid element; when sated or hungry, he also feels the liquid element's attributes. Man already feels the air element in his soul: he finds breathing difficult when the air's composition is not right and with breathing difficulty, angst. Warmth is something in which the human being feels completely immersed. He accompanies his cold and warm states with his whole I. Fire ignites the I.

The heart motivated by Christ answers:

Christ: My I blazes in God's fire, as long as the spirit ignites me.

Man does not need earthly-material warmth when the spirit enflames or ignites: the I blazes in divine fire, not in earthly warmth, not in earthly fire.

But the heart motivated by Lucifer answers:

My I has the power of flame through the spirit's solar force.

In immense pride the I – ensnared by Lucifer – wants to usurp for itself the fire element that comes from the sun, instead of only for the time the spirit sets it ablaze – keep it forever, never give it away.

Lucifer: My I has the force of flame through the spirit's solar power.

The heart motivated by Ahriman answers as though it wants to keep for itself the fire it had captured on earth and carry it over to the spiritual world – to master the spiritual world with the I-fire of the physical world.

Ahriman: My I has its own fire, which ignites through self-enfoldment.

The I wills not to blaze in the spirit, but to develop its own fire.

There is again an ascending direction in the formulation:

The person first says "I":

    I leave

    I feel

    I will

He then becomes more objective in that what is in him refers to "My":

> My life extinguishes
>
> My life melts
>
> My life solidifies.

He goes more within, what is within makes him objective:

> My soul breathes
>
> My soul cares not
>
> My soul absorbs it.

Now he delves deeper into himself. And – note the difference, my dear sisters and brothers – before only "I" was said. Now the "I" becomes objective: "My I", as though it were another, as if one were to speak of the other as a possession. One is more outside of the physical body – which disposes one to speak so egoistically of the "I" – and speaks:

> My I

as of an object. That is the correct speech here.

One gets to know this way of speaking in all its intensity, my dear sisters and brothers, when one speaks with souls who have passed through the gates of death and have been a while in the spiritual world. They never say "I", but they say "my I". I have not yet heard a dead person say "I" after death, at most only shortly after death. But after a certain time after death they always say "my I", for they see the I with the eyes of the gods. They become completely objective. It is characteristic. Therefore an enunciation from a dead person who has been dead a long time can never be true if he says "I" and not "my I". So the soul speaks this "my I" here in the fourth place when standing before the Guardian of the Threshold.

That, my dear friends, is the wonderful conversation at the threshold between the Guardian of the Threshold and the human being. It is distinctive. And this distinctiveness is really present when one stands before the Guardian of the Threshold in this situation. When one practices the meditation of this dialog in the right way, as has been described here, one must be able to intuitively hear it. Therefore we meditate these words correctly, which have come to you here today as mantric words, my dear sisters and brothers, when in a sense we hear ourselves speaking the words after the Guardian has been heard in our souls. Thus we meditate first hearing the Guardian of the Threshold four times as I, II, III and IV, as earth, water, air and fire; then as when we let our own soul answer, but in such a way that first we hear the answer innerly ensouled by Christ, the second answer as the voice of the tempter, the third answer as the voice of the inflated materialistic Ahriman-spirit, which approaches the human being with the desire to carry the mineralized human being into the spiritual world.

Therefore, to end this esoteric lesson today, the way this is to be meditated resounds in us:

> Where is the earth's solidity, which supported you?
> I leave its foundation, as long as the spirit supports me.
> I feel rapture, for from now on I do not need its support.
> I will hammer it down even harder with the spirit's power.
>
> Where is the water's formative force which pervaded you?
> My life extinguishes it, as long as the spirit forms me.
> My life melts it away, so I am released from it.
> My life solidifies it, so I transfer it to the spirit-realm.
>
> Where is the air's stimulating force, which awakened you?
> My soul breathes the air of heaven, as long as the spirit surrounds me.
> My soul regards it not in the spirit's rapture.
> My soul absorbs it, that I may learn divine creation.
>
> Where is fire's cleansing, which ignited your I?
> My I blazes in God's fire, as long as the spirit ignites me.
> My I has the force of flame through the spirit's solar power.
> My I has its own fire, which ignites through self-enfolding.

LESSON FIFTEEN

Dornach, June 21, 1924

My dear friends,

Today we will also begin with the mantric verse when rings out to human beings from all sides of cosmic events and cosmic beings, if they can truly understand with inner heart and soul what certain cosmic beings and events may tell them.

> O man, know thyself!
> So sounds the Cosmic-Word.
> You hear it strong in soul,
> You feel it firm in spirit.
>
> Who speaks with such cosmic might?
> Who speaks with such depth of heart?
>
> Does it work through distant radiant space
> Into your senses' sense of being?
> Does it ring through weaving waves of time
> Into your life's evolving stream?
>
> It's you yourself who,
> In feeling space, in experiencing time
>
> The Word create, feeling foreign
> In the soulless void of space,
> Because you lose the force of thought
> In time's destructive flow.

My dear sisters and brothers, my dear friends, because various Class members have come today who have not been present previously, it will be necessary to say certain things which, only for the sake of coherence, are necessary in order to grasp with full understanding what the content of these Class lessons are meant to be.

We have so far covered, my dear sisters and brothers, how the pictures of life appear before the soul when with real knowledge we approach the abyss which opens between the world in which we live, which surrounds us here, and that world in which we have our true being, our humanity.

We become aware, if we perceive the world around us correctly, how this world demands our intense attention. We look down at the lowest worms and up at the glowing, sparkling stars in the sky. We look all around at the kingdoms of nature, much of what is derived from them being part of us. And we have every reason to deeply feel in our hearts and souls the sublimity, the cosmic importance and the majesty of all this. And participation in any kind of esoteric, in any spiritual science, should not tempt us to engage in false asceticism – to reject either the lowly worm or the majestic stars because they belong to the visible world – and not feel their greatness, their majesty and sublimity, nor feel the importance they have for us.

As true adherents of spiritual science, we should feel that we are a part of the world around us. But we should also be aware – and we can be aware of it if we put our hearts and souls into the phenomena and beings and events of the world in the right way – we can and should be conscious of the fact that our true highest human self cannot be found in all the kingdoms of nature; that it cannot be found in the sunlit shining world, despite it's grandeur and nobility; that we must seek it in a world separated from our perception by an abyss; and that what is beyond that abyss in the world from which we really originate, appears to us at first as the blackest darkness. It stands like a wall before us, with the abyss in front of it.

The first being we encounter stands at this abyss. Every night when we sleep we find ourselves in the realm to which we belong with the most inner, true being of our humanity; we are really within it, that must be emphasized . But we may only consciously enter this realm in full maturity. The Guardian of the Threshold is there to warn us that we may not enter immaturely. He is the first spiritual being we meet if we have the earnest, real will to look into and to enter the world of our origin.

It is the Guardian of the Threshold himself who speaks the first words to us if we wish to take to path over the abyss into the realm of spirituality from which we originate. For it is the Guardian of the Threshold who first admonishes us to look back at our own self in order to seek the foundation of cosmic knowledge in self-knowledge.

This is all given in mantric verses for those who have participated in these lessons, and leads to what was put forth in the previous lesson.

Now we came to situational meditation: how to see ourselves already on the other side of the abyss, but still under the influence of the Guardian of the Threshold's admonishment, whose words enable us to understand our situation once we have flown over the abyss into the realm which at first is dark to us.

As long as we are here, in the realm in which we did *not* originate, we have the solidity of the earth under us – which bears and supports us, which we touch with our whole bodies when we are on it – the first, the earth-element.

We contain in us, by feeling what is called "water" in spiritual science, but which entails all liquidity which forms us, which makes us grow, from which all our organs are formed – the second, the water-element. The Guardian of the Threshold's admonishment also refers to this water-element, which is also the blood-element.

Regarding what we inhale through our breathing, the air-element, in regard to what we take in through warmth, through the active fire in us, the Guardian of the Threshold also directs important words to us.

And the cosmic powers act in us, in order that an answer forms in us to what the

Guardian of the Threshold is asking. This answer, which the cosmic-powers themselves activate in us, can come from Christ: then it will be the right answer. It can come from Lucifer: then it will be the wrong answer. It can come from Ahriman: then it will again be the wrong answer.

Christ's council will always be shaped in conjunction with each of the elements, so that we may feel ourselves to be completely in the spiritual world, completely in harmony with the spiritual element – but also so that we know that as long as we are earthly beings we must always return over the abyss as earthly beings and that we do not want the characteristics of the spiritual world to claim us longer than our presence in that spiritual world endures.

Christ will always speak to us, counseling: as long as we are in the spiritual world we should be one with this spiritual world; when we come back we should live as real earthly beings, for only with the spirit should we wish to be in the spiritual world.

Lucifer will always spur us on and tempt us to want to stay in the spiritual world, to merge with it, to merge with the feeling of wellbeing of the spiritual world.

Ahriman will always tempt us to enter into his service by dragging the spiritual world over into the physical.

We must let such things resonate in our souls so that we correctly feel the situation of the human being when he faces the spiritual world.

Therefore let us imagine that we are already in the spiritual world on the other side of the abyss, still in utter darkness. The Guardian of the Threshold is at the abyss, warning us with his right hand extended, asking us questions which cut deeply into our souls. We sense that to each question a threefold answer comes from us: Christ's answer, Lucifer's answer, Ahriman's answer.

The Guardian speaks:

Where is the earth's solidity, which supported you?

(There is no ground. We are in the spiritual world.)

Christ in us answers:

I abandon its ground, as long as the spirit bears me.

Lucifer in us answers:

I feel sweet and lovely, so I no longer need the ground.

Ahriman answers:

I will hammer it more firmly with the spirit's force.

The Guardian speaks:

Where is water's forming force, which pervaded you?

Christ in us answers:

My life dismisses it, as long as the spirit forms me.

Lucifer in us:

My life dissolves it, so I am released from it.

Ahriman in us speaks:

My life strengthens it, so I can carry it over into the spirit realm.

The Guardian speaks:

Where is air's energizing power, which awakened you?

Christ in us:

My soul breathes heavenly air, as long as the spirit surrounds me.

Lucifer in us:

My soul respects it not in the spirit's beatitude.

Ahriman in us:

My soul absorbs it, that I may learn divine creation.

The Guardian speaks:

Where is the fire's cleansing, that enflamed your I?

Christ in us:

My I blazes in divine fire, as long as the spirit kindles me.

Lucifer in us:

My I has the power of flame through the spiritual force of the sun.

Ahriman in us:

My I has its own fire, which flames purely through self-unfoldment.

We are tested by the Guardian's questions as to how we will comport ourselves in respect to the earth's firm support, to the formative force of the fluids in us, to the astrality of the creative forces of air in us, to the I-bearing force of fire in us. And Christ answers in us to correctly energize the humanity in us. Lucifer answers temptingly in us, as though we wished to adhere to the beatitude forever, which we should only possess during the moments we give ourselves over the the spirit. And Ahriman answers in us as though we wished to transfer to the realm of earth what we shared in the spirit-land.

We must let what is active in the soul be what is possible for the soul. We must not only expose ourselves to the voice of Christ, but also to those of Lucifer and Ahriman. In meditation we must imagine ourselves in this situation. Then, my dear sisters and brothers, because we are called in the innermost depths of soul, we will be liberated to the extent that, in this liberating spirit-experience, we can really make the spiritual element our own.

Today we must review this situation again. We must strongly feel ourselves on the other side of this threshold of the abyss, the warning Guardian of the Threshold at our side; in us the voices which pull human beings in different directions: Lucifer and Ahriman; the voice of Christ in us, which shows us the right direction, while Lucifer one one side and Ahriman on the other try to lead us into error. Then we will hold to the orientation which makes it possible to make a start in the spiritual world with the right feelings.

We can only achieve this, my dear sisters and brothers, if we gradually acquire the ability to feel about the higher spiritual beings as we do about the three kingdoms of nature here in the world of the senses.

When we stand here in the physical world, we feel outside of us the essence of stone, of the mineral kingdom, and we say: this mineral essence also exists in us. We have salt in us in which the mineral element exists, and which enables us to be human beings within the earthly realm.

We look at the world of plants. We know: we take into ourselves the being of plants, we have it in our earthly being within the confines of our skin, we bear it in our growth process, in all that forms our organism, also in all that we evolve in sleep. We feel the essence of plants in us as we observe the plants around us.

We look at the animals and know that we bear the essence of animality in our astrality, in our breathing process. We look at the immense variety of animals and say: we feel identified with this animality because we bear it in ourselves. Only we elevate it to the level of humanity.

Thus we find ourselves here in the sensible world standing among the three kingdoms of nature. We must also learn to feel when we are in the spirit-world among its beings with our spiritual-psychical humanity, as we feel when we are here with our etheric-physical humanity among the kingdoms of nature. Just as we must learn to be physical beings among other physical beings, so must we learn to be spirit-soul beings among other spirit-soul beings.

We have learned about the spirit-soul world, which touches us as men in the form of three hierarchies, just as we have learned to know the beings within the three kingdoms of nature. We belong to the three kingdoms of nature with our etheric-physical nature. We belong to the three kingdoms of the hierarchies with our spirit-soul being. When we are here in the sensible world it is natural for us to belong to the three kingdoms of nature and to let them flow through us, to be among them. When we are in the spirit-soul world, it must be natural for us to belong to that world and to the beings of the higher hierarchies for the time we have there, and to realize that we are among these beings of the higher hierarchies, just as we do in respect to the beings of the kingdoms of nature.

The Guardian indicates this to us again. And the mantric words, brought forth from the spiritual world through the magical force of the Guardian's voice, must resound repeatedly, again and again, in our souls in meditation. Then they will have the force, through the simple way they are formulated and the repetitions contained in them, to awaken in our souls the sensation of standing in the spiritual world among the hierarchies.

Therefore, we are to imagine the mantras which the Guardian now speaks in the following way. We are still in darkness on the other side of the threshold in the spiritual world. We first learn to feel in the spiritual world before we learn to see. The Guardian speaks again with respect to the elements – at first earth, water and air; fire will be the subject of the next lesson – So first the Guardian speaks about the earth, water and air elements, about everything in us which is solid; everything that is fluid in us, especially our blood and tissue fluids; about everything in us which is airy, the inhaled air. The Guardian speaks about all that. And he calls out what resounds from the world of the hierarchies.

After the Guardian has spoken to us, the hierarchies speak one after the other. The third hierarchy with the first mantra: first the Angeloi, then Archangeloi, and thirdly the Archai. We feel ourselves to be in this situation. The Guardian of the Threshold speaks to us. The words resound from out of the darkness, as if they came from under the earth, yet resounding deeply in our souls.

The Guardian speaks:

What becomes of the earth's solidity, which supported you?

The Angeloi from the third hierarchy:

Feel, as we feel in your thinking.

The Archangeloi from the third hierarchy:

Experience, as we experience in your feeling.

The Archai from the third hierarchy:

Perceive, as we perceive in your willing.

From the cosmos we are receiving an important threefold teaching about the Guardian of the Threshold's questions. His words call forth the answers from the Angeloi, the Archangeloi and the Archai with magical force.

What do the Angeloi teach us? We humans think. At first we believe that we are experiencing our thoughts alone. But as our thoughts are passing through our minds, the Angeloi really live in them. And when we feel with our senses – as when we grasp something – the Angeloi live in our thinking; it is their feeling. They bring it to our consciousness. And just as the Angeloi feel in our thinking, the Archangeloi experience in our feeling, and the Archai perceive in our willing.

When a thought is passing through your minds, my dear sisters and brothers, then feel that in this thought a being from the hierarchy of the Angeloi feels something. The Angeloi touch something when you think. When you are feeling, a being from the hierarchy of the Archangeloi experiences something. When you are willing, while your willing is unfolding, a being from the hierarchy of the Archai perceives something. Human thinking, human feeling, human willing, are not mere processes in humanity. While we are thinking, the Angeloi are feeling; while we are feeling, the Archangeloi are experiencing; while we are willing, the Archai are perceiving.

[The first part of the mantra is written on the blackboard – always in italics.]

The Guardian:

What becomes of the earth's solidity, which supported you?

From the hierarchy of the Angeloi [the answer] resounds:

Angeloi:

Feel, as we feel in your thinking.

From the hierachy of the Archangeloi resounds:

Archangeloi:

Experience, as we experience in your feeling.

From the hierarchy of the Archai resounds:

Archai:

Perceive, as we perceive in your willing.

This is what replaces the earth-element in the spiritual world. For the solidity of the earth is not there. The earth's ground is gone. Everything solid is gone. The third hierarchy of Angeloi, Archangeloi, Archai do not create solidity the way minerals do. In our thinking we would not only sink downward but to all directions if the Angeloi did not act in it, if it did not have their feeling in it. We would be thrown formlessly in all directions if the Archangeloi did not live in our feeling. We would disappear into nothing in our willing if we did not have the Archai's strengthen of perception in this willing.

Second is water, which provides us with formative force: the liquid element in us. Again we image that we are standing beyond the abyss in the spiritual world still in darkness. First we learn feeling. The Guardian speaks in admonishment, questioning. But now the beings of the second hierarchy, the Exusiai, Dynamis, Kyriotetes, answer about the force of fluids, the element of water.

The Guardian speaks:

What becomes of water's formative force, which pervaded you?

From the second hierarchy the Exusiai answer:

Know the spirit's-cosmic-creation in the human-body's-creation.

The Dynamis of the second hierarchy:

Feel the spirit's-cosmic-life in the human-body's-life.

The Kyriotetes of the second hierarchy:

Will the spirit's-cosmic-process in the human-body's-being.

By this means we become aware that in our surroundings we do not stand alone. We should learn to feel that in the physical existence within the boundaries of our skin lives a portion of cosmic being. The second hierarchy is in us, acts in us as though we were cosmic beings, beings which belong as members to the cosmos.

By means of these mantras, we should become aware that we stand within the cosmic process, and that everything, from the most minute vibrations of our cells to the powerful, sublime wave movement of our blood, to the rhythm of our breathing system, to the rhythm that allows day to change into night, that it is all not only a process in us, but is also part of the cosmic process.

[The second part of the mantra is written on the blackboard.]

The Guardian:

What becomes of the water's formative force, which pervaded you?

The Exusiai from the second hierarchy answer:

Exusiai:

Know the spirit's-cosmic-creation in the human-body's-creation.

The Dynamis from the second hierarchy answer:

Dynamis:

Feel the spirit's-cosmic-life in the human-body's-life.

The Kyriotetes from the second hierarchy answer:

Kyriotetes:

Will the spirit's-cosmic-process in the human-body's-being.

An exactness exists in these mantric verses. Therefore the question may arise: Why do we have here "body's-being" in contrast to "cosmic process"? We must feel each word exactly if a mantric verse is to work correctly in our souls. Outside of us the cosmic process carries on, in that we feel it to be a process. This cosmic-process is everywhere expanding, filling the universe. –

[Translator's note: The German word "Welt" can refer to world, cosmos/cosmic, or universe. With few exceptions, Rudolf Steiner always said "Welt". I have used the variation which I consider to best meet the requirements of his meaning.]

– In that it continues in us, is in us, we feel it to be an closed entity because we are enclosed within our skin and feel ourselves to be complete and enclosed. We do not feel everything within us as weaving, waving and undulating, as we do outside us. Therefore "process" and "being" are in contrast, whereas the repetitions "create" "create" and "life" "life" [in the previous lines] are correct.

In respect to the air-element, the Guardian of the Threshold raises his questions. The beings of the first hierarchy – Thrones, Cherubim, Seraphim – answer. They admonish us that we should be conscious of how the cosmos works in us. From merely being conscious, the beings of the first hierarchy lead us to being self-conscious.

The Guardian speaks:

What becomes of air's stimulating force, which awakened you?

The Thrones answer from the first hierarchy:

Knowingly grasp the inner-being in your divine-cosmic-being.

The Cherubim answer from the first hierarchy:

Warm the inner-life in your divine-cosmic-life.

The Seraphim answer from the first hierarchy:

Waken within inner-light in your divine-cosmic-light.

Now we are exhorted to waken self-consciousness at a higher level, in that we have felt our merging in the cosmos, our dedication to the cosmos, through the magical words of the second hierarchy.

[The third part of the mantra is written on the blackboard.]

The Guardian:

What becomes of the air's stimulating force, which awakened you?

The cosmic answer resounds from the first hierarchy:

Thrones:

Knowingly grasp the inner-being in your divine-cosmic-being.

Cherubim:

Warm the inner-life in your divine-cosmic-life.

Seraphim:

Awaken within inner-light in your divine-cosmic-light.

Yes, my dear sisters and brothers, if we do not feel the effect of this last mantra, how it resounds from the fiery, lightning-strong Seraphim: "Awaken within inner-light in your divine-cosmic-light", how these fiery words resound from the flaming lightning of the Seraphim, we will not sense how a force must awaken in our own souls with which, where we are standing in darkness beyond the abyss, still trying to orient ourselves, we feel the universe gradually approaching us – so that by and by a glimmer emerges, then becoming lighter, a continual expansion of the glimmer in space. And as the glimmer grows more glowing and shining, and through our own power the night-enveloped darkness beyond in the spiritual world gradually gets lighter. That is how it must be. We must try to develop the kindling force of our own selves, the kindling fiery force of our own humanity – for it is light in what was at first a night-enveloped spiritual land.

Thus we feel integrated in that threefold spirit-world of the Angeloi, Exusiai, Thrones and so forth, just as we feel integrated here in the sensible world of the three kingdoms of nature. And we learn as truly human to feel at home in spiritual surroundings just as sense-perceptible beings we feel at home in sense-perceptible surroundings. We learn as we ascend from the third hierarchy – who unfold the spirit in us, our own spirit, in which they live – to the second hierarchy, who develop the spirit in us, creating, living, shaping; and finally to the first hierarchy, where we again have support, but support of spirit, which is above and not below, where we have the mighty wisdom of the Cherubim who bring to our self-consciousness what can warm our inner life with self-knowledge, self-feeling, self-warming – and this warmed self becomes the shining-element, so that what was previously dark for us becomes light.

Thus we are standing at the Guardian of the Threshold's side deeply feeling that admonition which resounds from all the cosmic beings, from all the cosmic events, so that we can gain from self-knowledge cosmic-knowledge, and from cosmic-knowledge human-knowledge, so that we can stand in the realm of nature, but also in the realm of spirit, and realize our Self from both sides of reality: from the side of nature and from the side of the spirit.

Then a new form resounds – not different in words, but in our feeling, strengthened by the admonishments from all the hierarchies of the spiritual world, from which we originated.

> O man, know thyself!
> So sounds the Cosmic-Word.
> You hear it strong in soul,

You feel it firm in spirit.

Who speaks with such cosmic might?
Who speaks with such depth of heart?

Does it work through distant radiant space
Into your senses' sense of being?
Does it ring through weaving waves of time
Into your life's evolving stream?

It's you yourself who,
In feeling space, in experiencing time

The Word create, feeling foreign
In the soulless void of space,
Because you lose the force of thought
In time's destructive flow.

———————

LESSON SIXTEEN

Dornach, June 28, 1924

My dear friends,

We will again start by letting the words resound from the cosmos near and far, which can be heard by everyone who correctly understands the world. But before doing so, because again many new members of the esoteric school are present, I must say at least a few words about the meaning of this school.

I will put it briefly. This School must be recognized as one which brings down its information from the spiritual world to human souls. Therefore what lives here in the School and what is brought to human souls are to be perceived as communications from the spiritual world itself. From this you will understand that membership in the School must be regarded as serious in the highest degree.

This seriousness has only become possible because of the Constitution which the Anthroposophical Society received during the Christmas Conference. Since then the Anthroposophical Society as such is an openly public institution, but at the same time one through which an esoteric breath flows, which has been better received than the former exoteric one.

So nothing more is expected from the members of the Anthroposophical Society than that they feel themselves to be receivers of anthroposophical wisdom. And, of course, what is generally expected of decent people in life.

But membership in the School implies even more, that the member recognize the serious conditions for membership – namely the basic condition that anyone who wishes to belong to the School should present himself in life in such a way that he is in every respect a representative of Anthroposophy before the world.

To be a representative of Anthroposophy before the world necessarily means that whatever he or she does in connection to Anthroposophy, be it ever so remotely connected, also be with the approval of the leadership of the School, that is, with the esoteric Executive Committee at the Goetheanum. Thus through the School a real stream can enter the anthroposophical movement, which today is represented by the Anthroposophical Society.

Therefore, it is necessary that membership in the School be understood in such a way that the member feels in his whole being that he is a part of what is being done and revealed from here in the Goetheanum. Such a condition should not be taken as a restriction on human freedom, my dear friends, for membership in the school rests on reciprocity. The leadership of the School must be free to give what it has to give to whom it considers right to do so. And the fact that no one is obliged to be a member of the School, but that it depends on his free will to be a member, means that the leadership may also place conditions on membership without anyone claiming that his free will is in any way infringed upon. It is a free agreement between the leadership of the School and those who wish to be members.

Furthermore, in order that the School really be taken seriously, it cannot be otherwise than that the leadership exercise its right to revoke a membership whenever it considers necessary because of certain events. And, my dear friends, that the leadership of the School takes this seriously is shown by the fact that since the relatively short time the School has existed, sixteen members already had to be suspended for shorter or longer lengths of time. And I must again emphasize that this measure will have to be strictly adhered to in the future, regardless of the personalities involved, because we will be entering ever more deeply into esoteric matters.

* * *

And now the words will be spoken which are always spoken at the beginning of our deliberations, reminding us of the admonitions which resound from all the events and beings of the world to all those who have the heart to understand them: the admonition to self-knowledge, which is the true foundation of world knowledge.

> O man, know thyself!
> So resounds the Cosmic-Word.
> You hear it strong in soul,
> You feel it firm in spirit.
>
> Who speaks with such cosmic might?
> Who speaks with such depth of heart?
>
> Does it work through distant radiant space
> Into your senses' sense of being?
> Does it ring through weaving waves of time
> Into your life's evolving stream?
>
> It's you yourself who,
> In feeling space, in experiencing time
>
> The Word create, feeling foreign
> In the soulless void of space,
> Because you lose the force of thought
> In time's destructive flow.

My dear friends, we have advanced, in respect to what has been sent to us from the spiritual world in the form of mantras, to the mantric verses which correspond to the esoteric situation in which we feel ourselves: first of all, in meditation we imagine the being standing at the abyss of existence speaking to us.

Let us imagine it once more, for we cannot recall it to our souls too often. We see before us everything belonging to the kingdoms of nature. We observe the glorious heavenly bodies; we see the floating clouds; we see the wind and the waves, the thunder and lightning. We see everything from the humblest worm to the most sublime revelations in the glittering stars. Only a false asceticism, unrelated to true esotericism, could in any way despise this world that speaks to the senses. The person who wishes to be truly human can do nothing other than intimately relate to the sense-perceptible life, from the humblest creature to the majestic, divinely glittering stars.

We must never despise the grandeur and awesome beauty of all that surrounds us, which we must acknowledge; we must go forward step by step in the world and be able to appreciate what our eyes see, what our ears hear, what the other senses perceive, what we can grasp with our reason. However, a moment comes as you look around at the expanse of space, at the interweaving of time, that despite all the grandeur and awesome beauty in your surroundings, you cannot find there what the inner nature of your being is. So you must say to yourself: the inner source of my being is to be sought elsewhere. The very power of such a thought affects us.

What follows for the soul can only be expressed in imaginative thoughts. At first these imaginative thoughts lead us to a wide field in which everything earthly and sense-perceptible is spread out before us. We find it to be radiant with the sun, we find it to be shining light. But as we look all around us we find our own self nowhere. Then we gaze before us and see that this sunny field, which is grandiose and beautiful and sublime to the senses, is blocked by a dark, night-bedecked wall. We see ourselves entering deeply into the darkness. We intuit that perhaps there in the darkness is our self's true origin; but we cannot see into it.

And as we follow the path forward, the abyss of existence, the threshold to the spiritual world, appears before us. We must cross over this abyss. The Guardian stands there warning us that we must be mature in order to cross over the abyss, for with our thinking, feeling and willing habits which correspond to the physical sense-perceptible world, we cannot cross over the abyss of existence into the spiritual world in which our real self originated.

The Guardian of the Threshold is the first spiritual being we encounter. Every night we are in this spiritual world when we sleep. But it is like darkness around our I and our astral body, because we can only enter this spiritual world when sufficiently mature. The Guardian of the Threshold protects us from entering immaturely. But now as we encounter him he sends us his grand admonishments. And the admonishments are contained in the mantric verses which until now have formed the content of these esoteric lessons.

Those of you who do not yet have these mantric verses can obtain them from other members of the School. But the following procedure must be observed: not the person who is to receive the verses asks for permission, but the one who gives them.

These verses have not only shown us how our hearts are to react if we wish to cross over the abyss of existence, they have also shown us what our souls will feel once we have overflown the abyss and gradually sense – not yet see, but sense – how the darkness, which was at first night-bedecked, gradually becomes lighter. At first we feel becoming lighter, and we feel that the elements – earth, water, air, fire – are different on the other side, that we are living in another world. And the world in which we recognize our own being, and therewith the true form of the elements, is indeed another world.

During the last lesson we considered the meditation with which we were to imagine how the Guardian stands before the abyss of existence; now we are already beyond it, first we feel – not yet see – how the darkness becomes lighter. The Guardian speaks to us, after he had previously made clear to us how we should comport ourselves in relation to the four elements. He tells us how these four elements change for us. He then asks questions.

Who answers? The hierarchies themselves answer these questions. From one side the third hierarchy – Angeloi, Archangeloi, Archai – from the other side the second hierarchy, from a third side the third hierarchy.

The third hierarchy – Angeloi, Archangeloi, Archai – answers when the Guardian of the Threshold asks what becomes of the earth's solidity. The second hierarchy – Exusiai, Dynamis, Kyriotetes – answers when the Guardian of the Threshold asks us what becomes of the water's formative force, which acts in us and gives us our inner configuration. And the first hierarchy – Thrones, Cherubim, Seraphim – answer when the Guardian asks us what becomes of our breathing, of the air's stimulating power, which awakens us from dull plant-like existence to sentient-feeling existence.

Such mantras are to penetrate our souls, our hearts, to the extent that we feel ourselves to be within the situation. The Guardian of the Threshold poses the testing, admonishing questions. The hierarchies answer.

The Guardian: What becomes of the earth's solidity, which supports you?

Angeloi:

Feel as we feel in your thinking.

Archangeloi:

Experience, as we experience in your feeling.

Archai:

Perceive, as we perceive in your will.

The Guardian:

What becomes of water's formative force, which penetrated you?

Exusiai:

Learn the spirit cosmic creating in the human body creating.

Dynamis:

Feel the cosmic life of spirit in the human body's life.

Kyriotetes:

Will the spirit's cosmic working in the human body's being.

The Guardian:

What becomes of the air's stimulating power, which awakened you?

Thrones:

Knowingly grasp inner being in your divine cosmic being.

Cherubim:

Warm your inner life in divine cosmic life.

Seraphim:

Awaken inner light in your divine cosmic light.

These, my dear sisters and brothers, are the admonishing words coming from the communion of the Guardian of the Threshold together with the hierarchies, which bring our souls ever forward if we experience them more and more in the right way.

In this way, we are doing what is appropriate for human beings of today and the future, what in the ancient holy mysteries meant that the student was being guided to the essence of the elements: earth, water, air.

But warmth, which is also an element, pervades everything: in the solid earth element, which supports us, is warmth; in the element of water, which forms us as humans, which gives form to our organs, causing them to develop and grow, warmth is also present; and in the element of air, by which the Jehovah-spirits once breathed into humanity its soul, through which man is even today awakened from his dull, plant-like existence, warmth is present. Warmth is everywhere. We must recognize it as the all-pervading element. We must immerse ourselves in it as the all-pervading element: Yes, we feel so close to it.

We feel far from the solid earth element, though we still feel the earth's support. We even feel far from the water element. The air element maintains a more intimate relation to us. When the air element does not fill us with regularity, when we have too much breath in us, or too little, our inner life indicates how the air-element is connected to us. Too much breath awakens fear in the soul. Too little causes fainting. Our soul is embraced by the air element.

We feel ourselves most intimately united with the warmth element. We ourselves are what is warm or cold in us. In order to live we must generate a certain amount of warmth. We are intimately close to the warmth element. If we want to be closer to it, then not only one hierarchy can speak, then the reminding words must resound together from various hierarchies.

Therefore, when the Guardian of the Threshold asks questions of us concerning the warmth element, the answers from the cosmos are different. The Guardian asks the question:

What becomes of fire's purification, which kindled your I?

We already know this question; it is the question about our entrance into the element of warmth, or fire. But now the answer does not come from one hierarchy or from a rank of one of the hierarchies, but the answer comes in choir from the Angeloi, the Exusiai, the Thrones; secondly the Archangeloi, Dynamis, Cherubim answer the Guardian's question; and thirdly Archai, Kyriotetes, Seraphim answer. Thus the three answers about the general nature of warmth resound from the choir-like words of the three hierarchies.

Therefore we are to imagine that when we hear the Guardian of the Threshold's warning reminders, the answers, which resound from our I, but which are stimulated by the hierarchies – come from all sides: first Angeloi, Exusiai, Thrones; secondly speak the Archangeloi, Dynamis, Cherubim; and thirdly speak Archai, Kyriotetes, Seraphim. All three hierarchies always speak: a rank from each of the three hierarchies always speaks. Thus the answers comes to us from the cosmos.

The Guardian speaks:

What becomes of the fire's purification, which kindled your I?

Angeloi, Exusiai, Thrones:

Awaken in the cosmic etheric vastness the flaming script of life.

From all three hierarchies we are reminded that everything which happened to us during earthly life is recorded in the cosmic ether and we see it recorded there when we have passed through the gate of death. Once we have passed through the gate of death, looking back at our earthly life, but also gazing out at the etheric vastness, what we have done and accomplished in thoughts, feelings and deeds during earthly life is recorded. It is your life's flaming script.

Archangeloi, Dynamis, Cherubim – answer in us:

Create the soul's atoning forces in circling waves of time.

We are admonished during the second stage we go through after passing through the gate of death, where we experience in reverse, in mirror images – that is, in its just atonement – what we have done here on earth. If we have harmed another human being in any way, we experience in the reverse stream of time what the other felt because of us. As I have said, the Archangeloi, Dynamis and Cherubim admonish us in this second stage, which we pass through between death and a new birth.

What our karma works through during the third stage – what happens when as souls we cooperate with other human souls and with the beings of the higher hierarchies

– the Archai (primal powers), Kyriotetes and Seraphim admonish us:

Ask help from the redemptive eternal force of spirit.

We must feel ourselves completely within this situation: the speaking Guardian of the Threshold – his earnest gesture toward us, his admonishment. And from the cosmic vastness, resounding, grasping our heart – what connects us with the riddle of life.

[The fourth part of the mantra is written on the blackboard.]

The Guardian speaks:

What becomes of fire's purification, which kindled your I?

Angeloi, Exusiai, Thrones:

Awaken in the cosmic etheric vastness the flaming script of life.

Archangeloi, Dynamis, Cherubim – they answer in us:

Create the soul's atoning forces in circling waves of time.

Archai, Kyriotetes, Seraphim:

Ask help from the redemptive eternal force of spirit.

What previously stood before us like a black, night-enclosed darkness, is not yet illuminated by light for the soul's eye. But we have the feeling that while we are standing within this black, night enclosed darkness, wherever we reach out we begin to feel a glimmering light. And we find ourselves in the situation where we know that we ourselves are within this glimmering light. We feel ourselves moving toward the Guardian of the Threshold. We had only seen him as long as we were in the field of the senses. Then we stepped into the darkness and heard his questioning, admonishing words.

But these admonishing, questioning words had led us to where we now feel something like a mild weaving, moving light. In this weaving, moving light we make our way to the Guardian of the Threshold seeking help. It is a unique experience: not yet light, but the light is making itself felt; in this felt light the Guardian of the Threshold, manifesting himself, as though he were becoming more intimate with us, as though he were leaning more to us now, as though we were also stepping closer to him.

And what he now says seems as though in [earthly] life a person is whispering something confidential in our ear. And what were at first admonishing, earnest words, trumpet-like, powerful, majestic, from all sides of the cosmos coming to our hearts, continues now as an intimate conversation with the Guardian of the Threshold in weaving, moving light. For now it is as though he no longer just speaks to us, it is as though he whispers to us:

Has your spirit understood?

Our inner self becomes warm when the Guardian of the Threshold says in confidence: "Has your spirit understood?" Our inner self becomes warm. It experiences itself in the warmth. And this inner self feels obliged to answer with devotion, quietly and humbly.   Thus   we   imagine   it   in   meditation:

The cosmic spirit in me

It held its breath within

And may its presence still

Illuminate my I.

[Der Weltengeist in mir

Er hielt den Atem an

Und seine Gegenwart

Mög' erleuchten mein Ich.]

Our I does not answer the question "Has your spirit understood?" with pride and arrogance: "I have understood", but the I feels: divine being streams through the innermost essence of the human being; it is divine breath in man which quietly lingers and prepares us for understanding.

[The first part of the new mantra is written on the blackboard.]

> *The Guardian:*
>
> *Has your spirit understood?*
>
> *The I:*
>
> *The cosmic spirit in me*
>
> *It held its breath within*
>
> *And may its presence still*
>
> *Illuminate my I.*

Secondly, the Guardian in confidence asks:

Has your soul apprehended?

The I answers:

The cosmic souls in me

Lived in the council of stars

And may their harmonies

Resounding create my I.

Again it is not proudly that the I is tempted to answer when the Guardian asks: Has your soul apprehended? Rather is the soul becoming aware that in it speaks the cosmic souls of the beings of the higher hierarchies, and that in what they say not an individual entity is present, but an entire council, a consultative meeting, as if the planets of a planetary system were circling and contributing their respective illuminating forces. Thus do the cosmic souls send their concise suggestions. Our soul hears and hopes that from the harmonies the I will be so formed that the I in the human being is an echo of the cosmic harmonies which arise when cosmic souls take council among each other – like the planets in the solar system – and their advice and harmonies resound in the human soul.

[The second part of the mantra is written on the blackboard.]

The Guardian:

Has your soul apprehended?

The I:

The cosmic souls in me

Lived in the council of stars

And may their harmonies

Resounding create my I.

And the third confidential question which the Guardian directs to the person in this situation is this:

Has your body experienced?

The soul feels that in this body the cosmic forces – which are everywhere – are concentrated in one point in space. But these cosmic forces do not appear now as physical forces. The soul has long since become aware of how these forces, which from outside appear as active physical forces, as gravitational, electrical, magnetic forces, as warmth forces, as light forces, when they are active in the human body are moral forces, are transformed into will-forces. The soul feels the cosmic forces as those which constitute eternal universal justice throughout the succession of earth lives. The soul feels them to be like forces of judgment which weave in the verdicts of karma and therewith the I itself.

When the Guardian asks in confidence:

Has your body experienced?

The human being feels obliged to answer with devotion to universal justice:

The cosmic forces in me

They judge the acts of men

And may their words of verdict

Guide the I in me.

[The third part of the mantra is written on the blackboard.]

The Guardian:

Has your body experienced?

I:

The cosmic forces in me

They judge the acts of men

And may their words of verdict

Guide the I in me.

Thus after having experienced the metamorphoses of the cosmic elements together with the Guardian of the Threshold and the hierarchies, the soul answers the Guardian's three questions with inner devotion; interwoven with what has been poured into it, the soul has advanced somewhat in answering the riddle of the words: "O man, know thyself!"

And today we will compare the opening words after having been filled with the element of warmth in devotion to the spiritual content of the cosmos, feeling how we have advanced further in following the great admonishment: "O man, know thyself!" We will see how we, as human beings, stand between the resounding of the demand for self-knowledge from all the cosmic events and beings, and the mantric verse, which has been contemplated in today's lesson:

O man, know thyself!
So resounds the Cosmic-Word.
You hear it strong in soul,
You feel it firm in spirit.

Who speaks with such cosmic might?
Who speaks with such depth of heart?

Does it work through distant radiant space
Into your senses' sense of being?
Does it ring through weaving waves of time
Into your life's evolving stream?

It's you yourself who,
In feeling space, in experiencing time

The Word create, feeling foreign
In the soulless void of space,
Because you lose the force of thought

In time's destructive flow.

What becomes of fire's purification, which enkindled your I?
Awaken in the cosmic etheric vastness the flaming script of life.
Create the soul's atoning forces in circling waves of time.
Ask help from the redemptive eternal force of spirit.

*

Has your spirit understood?

The cosmic spirit in me
It held its breath within
And may its presence still
Illuminate my I.

Has your soul apprehended?

The cosmic souls in me
Lived in the council of stars
And may their harmonies
Resounding create my I.

Has your body experienced?

The cosmic forces in me
They judge the acts of men
And may their words of verdict
Guide the I in me.

LESSON SEVENTEEN

Dornach, July 5, 1924

My dear Friends,

We also begin today with that verse which, by a correct understanding of the universe, resounds to human hearts from all that is and all that is becoming as a call to self-knowledge, which one must first attain for true knowledge of the cosmos.

    O man, know thyself!
    So resounds the Cosmic-Word.
    You hear it strong in soul,
    You feel it firm in spirit.

    Who speaks with such cosmic might?
    Who speaks with such depth of heart?

    Does it work through distant radiant space
    Into your senses' sense of being?
    Does it ring through weaving waves of time
    Into your life's evolving stream?

    It's you yourself who,
    In feeling space, in experiencing time

    The Word create, feeling foreign
    In the soulless void of space,
    Because you lose the force of thought
    In time's destructive flow.

Once more let us review in our souls what summarized the contents of the previous Class Lesson. It was also a meditation arising from what the human being can experience when he feels himself completely immersed in the cosmic context, above all in the context of the spiritual world.

Man's path to the abyss of existence, at which the Guardian of the Threshold stands, appeared before our souls. We heard the teachings the Guardian gives to those who cross the threshold. We heard how the person who arrives on the other side of the threshold at first feels himself to be within light, and experiences the world in a new way in that he first hears what the Guardian says, but also what the beings of the higher hierarchies are saying. In the last dialog the Guardian asks a question and the Angeloi,

Exusiai, Thrones; Archangeloi, Dynamis, Cherubim; Archai, Kyriotetes, Seraphim speak, one after the other, about the element of warmth, which penetrates everything and reveals itself to be a moral element on the other side of the abyss.

We saw how the Guardian then speaks to the I, asking three questions which penetrate deeply into the human being, and the I answers with humility, as was explained last time, but exchanging words as in a deeply intimate conversation with the Guardian.

The Guardian speaks:

What becomes of the fire's purification, which kindled your I?

Angeloi, Exusiai, Thrones:

Awaken in the cosmic etheric vastness the flaming script of life.

Archangeloi, Dynamis, Cherubim:

Create the soul's atoning forces in circling waves of time.

Archai, Kyriotetes, Seraphim:

Ask help from the redemptive eternal force of spirit.

The Guardian: Has your spirit understood?

The I:

The cosmic spirit in me

It held its breath within

And may its presence now

Illuminate my I.

The Guardian: Has your soul apprehended?

The I:

The cosmic souls in me

Lived in the council of stars

And may their harmonies

Resounding create my I.

The Guardian: Has your body experienced?

The I:
The cosmic forces in me
They judge the acts of men
And may their words of verdict
Guide the I in me.

The human being beyond the threshold of existence, where the Guardian stands, feels himself to be within weaving, living light. Gradually it becomes not only felt light, but a kind of light about which we can say that he sees it.

From feeling the light in waves, as in spiritual thoughts, so to speak, light appears which is seen by the spirit's eye.

But the human being cannot enter already seeing into this light without hearing another deeply founded admonition from the Guardian. And this admonition refers to a powerful cosmic imagination, something tremendously majestic which the person, even while being here in the sensible world, can receive as an impression – if he has the heart for it. For, when he becomes magically illuminated by the cloud formations and the majestic rainbow, then he can feel as if the spirits beyond the physical sense-perceptible rainbow's glow are shining in through its colors. It is there, builds itself up from the universe, then disappears back into the universe, is placed within the universe like a mighty imagination.

The Guardian reminds us of this rainbow's impression at the moment when it becomes light enough for perception there in the spiritual world.

[The rainbow is drawn on the blackboard.]

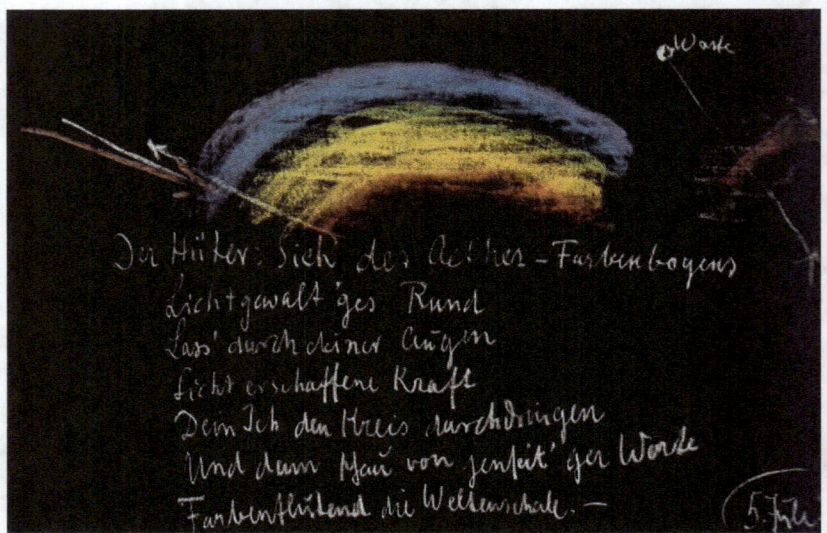

Blackboard Drawing for Lesson Seventeen

And the Guardian reminds us that the one who has come over to the spiritual world should recall the impression from the sensory world which the rainbow had made. For it is remarkable, my dear sisters and brothers, that when we cross over from the physical sensory world to the spiritual world, the image of the rainbow is the easiest to remember and the one which most easily allows us to recall the relationship between the spiritual world, where it is becoming light, and the physical-sensory world, which we have left together with our capacities for knowledge.

Not referring to the view of the rainbow itself, but to the memory of the rainbow which has been called forth by the Guardian of the Threshold, the Guardian now indicates (we will hear the exact words): Try, with the force you normally use to see with your eyes, to prepare the substance with which you will penetrate this rainbow, with which you will pass below, through the rainbow and to the other side.

If we can imagine [the second drawing is made]: here in the cloud formation [white in the upper right-hand corner] – looking up from the earth [small arrow] – the rainbow would be here [red in the cloud formation]. Then the Guardian instructs us to penetrate through that rainbow and from this vantage point [a line is drawn to the small circle on which the word "Warte" (vantage point) is written] which is on the other side, to look back from that cosmic distance at the rainbow. The Guardian instructs us to make our imagination more profound through meditation, if we wish to advance beyond the point we reached during the previous lesson.

When we look back from out there, if you imagine that you go behind the blackboard [white arrow pointing up and left in the first drawing], then look at the rainbow from behind [red arrow pointing down and left in the first drawing], as it appears in memory, looking from behind, then the rainbow becomes a powerful bowl, a cosmic bowl. And we no longer see a bow, we see a powerful bowl extending over half the sky, within which the colors flow into each other.

This is the imagination which the Guardian first introduces:

> See the ether-rainbow arc's
>
> Light teeming round,
>
> Let the light creating force
>
> Pass through your eyes,
>
> Your I penetrate the circle,
>
> Observe from the other side's vantage point
>
> Color flooding the cosmic bowl.

[This first stanza of the mantra is written on the blackboard.]

> *See the ether-rainbow arc's*
>
> *Light teeming round,*
>
> *Let the light creating force*
>
> *Pass through your eyes,*
>
> *Your I penetrate the circle,*
>
> *Observe from the other side's vantage point*
>
> *Color flooding the cosmic bowl.*

These are the powerful words spoken by the Guardian, my dear sisters and brothers, and you must put yourself correctly in the image-filled situation in which the Guardian of the Threshold's pupil finds himself when he is called to observe the cosmic bowl with its content of color-flooding light.

> See the ether-rainbow arc's
>
> Light teeming round,
>
> Let the light creating force
>
> Pass through your eyes,
>
> Your I penetrate the circle,

> Observe from the other side's vantage point
>
> Color flooding the cosmic bowl.

We must pass through such images. And if they work deeply into the I, then we see how the beings of the third hierarchy – Angeloi, Archangeloi, Archai – appear in the flood of colors that fill the bowl. They are breathing the colors into their own angelic beings.

Thus we have an idea about the cosmic creation behind the sensory world, which is the result of the deeds of the higher hierarchies; we have a conception of how the spiritual beings act beyond the rainbow, at first breathing in the cosmic bowl's colors, taking them into their own being.

We observe how what flows from the cosmos to the rainbow, penetrating it, then appears behind the rainbow as thoughts, how it is absorbed, breathed in by the angelic beings. Now we learn the true nature of the rainbow. All the thoughts thought by people in a particular place are gathered from time to time through the rainbow's bridge and sent farther out to the spiritual domain, where it is breathed in by the beings of the third hierarchy.

What so magically appears [the rainbow] in the vastness of the universe does not only have a physical meaning; it has a spiritual-inner meaning. And the magical ether-rainbow cannot be discerned from within the physical-sensory world; we can discern it only beyond the threshold of existence, once we have heard the Guardian of the Threshold's various admonitions.

Through the impression we receive from that outlook point of the rainbow as the cosmic bowl, it becomes clear to us how the light, which at first was a dark, night-bedecked sphere, spreads out before us. We are now within it. It brightens: it is sun, the cosmic bowl with its flood of colors seen from the other side of the rainbow.

Then the Angeloi, Archangeloi and Archai begin to reflect their consciousness within the human soul of how they breathe in the floods of color in order that what exists here on the earth as sense-perceptible may be brought into the spiritual domain, to the extent it is of use there.

And then we perceive how the beings of the third hierarchy have breathed in what they took from the sensible world, what has penetrated them through the rainbow, what they have transformed to the extent that it can be taken into the spiritual world – they go as helpers, with what they have absorbed within themselves, to the even higher spirits, to the spirits of the second hierarchy. For the spirits of the third hierarchy, Angeloi, Archangeloi, Angeloi, are the helping spirits of the spirit-world. We now hear from them what we see when we behold the color-flooded cosmic bowl – somewhere beyond the rainbow.

> Angeloi, Archangeloi, Archai:

Sense our thoughts

Breathing the colors of life

To the light-flooded bowl;

We carry the mirage of the senses

To spirit's domain of being

And turn, by the world inspired

To serve the higher spirits.

[This second stanza is written on the blackboard.]

Angeloi, Archangeloi, Archai:

Sense our thoughts

Breathing the colors of life

To the light-flooded bowl;

We carry the mirage of the senses

To spirit's domain of being

And turn, by the world inspired,

To serve the higher spirits.

My dear sisters and brothers, let us place the image once more before our souls: the cosmic bowl, half the sky in size, the colors flooding within – which we normally see toned down in the rainbow – weaving, living in one another; the beings of the third hierarchy, Angeloi, Archangeloi, Archai, approach. They breathe these colors. The thoughts of the beings of the third hierarchy are visible to us in this breathing of colors.

We observe how these beings of the third hierarchy, permeated with these cosmic thoughts, turn to the beings of the second hierarchy, the Exusiai, Dynamis, Kyriotetes, whom they serve. And we have this powerful image before us – the pure spirit-beings appear, the residents of the sun, who only appear when the physical image which the sun casts, disappears; for despite all its greatness in comparison to the earth, it is a small image – for it is only an image. And the sun majestically fills the entire universe, infinitely larger than the gigantic cosmic image. Then the beings of the second hierarchy appear, weaving, living in the pure spirit-domain, but now receiving what the Angeloi,

Archangeloi and Archai bring them. These are not dead thoughts, such as we have. The dead thoughts are taken from the illusion of the senses and become living thoughts through the breath of the Angeloi, Archangeloi, Archai. As a powerful offering, the Angeloi, Archangeloi, Archai place these living thoughts before the second hierarchy, the Exusiai, Dynamis, Kyriotetes. The thoughts which are illusions in earthly life are awakened to existence by the beings of the second hierarchy.

And we see how the beings of the second hierarchy receive from the beings of the third hierarchy the thoughts already made living by them; and we see that a powerful resurrection of a new world takes place, created out of what was dead, illusionary, and taken up by the Angeloi, Archangeloi, Archai. Thus a new world, a resurrecting world comes into existence through the workings of the Exusiai, Dynamis, Kyriotetes.

Then we see how the remarkable secret of the cosmos works. We see how the Exusiai, Dynamis, Kyriotetes give over what they received from the beings of the third hierarchy to what we call *rays* in earthly life – rays of the sun, of the stars. The awakened, now living world-thoughts are given over to all that rays.

In reality rays are not physical. In reality it is the spirit that beams in the rays. But we fail to see, when the rays reach us, what they had previously been given from the realm of the beings of the second hierarchy. All these rays, the rays of the stars, the rays of the sun, have been given what the beings of the second hierarchy weave in world-thoughts, but also what they let be resurrected from the dead thoughts – our thoughts on earth – which were made living by the beings of the third hierarchy. And now we hear how they also give to these raying spiritual forces what works as creative love in the cosmos – what weaves in the sun and star rays as love; the love that floods the cosmos and which is the creative force in the whole cosmos; how they entrust it to the rays of the stars, to the rays of the sun. We now see with the eye of the spirit how the beings of the second hierarchy – raying spirit, awakening love, bearing love – merge with the world.

Thus we hear them speaking, not to us; we are witnesses to a dialog between the beings of the second hierarchy and the beings of the third hierarchy. It resounds across. We only listen. It is the first time in the course of situational meditation that we hear the beings of the hierarchies speaking to each other:

> What you have received
>
> From dead illusion made live:
>
> We waken it to existence;
>
> We give it to the rays,
>
> Who manifest with love
>
> The nothingness of matter
>
> In the spirit's essence.

By being witnesses to a heavenly dialog, the once night-bedecked darkness is gradually illuminated for the eye of the spirit. It becomes filled with a soft, mild light.

[The third stanza is written on the blackboard.]

> *What is received by you*
>
> *From dead illusion made live:*
>
> *We awaken it to existence;*
>
> *We give it to the rays,*
>
> *Who manifest with love*
>
> *the nothingness of matter*
>
> *In the spirit's essence.*

If we have heard and have absorbed all this, then we will see with the spirit's eye something else taking place. We have already seen how earthly thoughts are made living ones by the third hierarchy, that what was made living is received by the second hierarchy and then shared with the rays of the stars and with the rays of the sun, and transformed into love. Now we see it taken over by the beings of the first hierarchy and made by these beings into the elements with which to create new worlds; what Angeloi, Archangeloi, Archai breathe in from the world, what Exusiai, Dynamis, Kyriotetes receive from them and transform into creative forces from which they – Thrones, Cherubim, Seraphim – shape new worlds.

What is remarkable is this: first we were witnesses to a conversation in heaven between the beings of the third and second hierarchies. Then we hear more with our spiritual ears. The beings of the first hierarchy begin to speak the cosmic words. At first it seems as though we were only to be listeners to a heavenly conversation. But soon we realize that it is not so.

First the Angeloi, Archangeloi, Archai made their voices heard; then a dialog took place between the Exusiai, Dynamis, Kyriotetes and the Angeloi, Archangeloi, Archai; then the Thrones, Cherubim, Seraphim join the conversation. A choir of the spiritual spheres rings out. We become aware, now that the voices of all nine choirs ring out together, that what they are intoning is directed at us as human beings. And so finally the whole spirit world speaks to us. But only when what has been spoken within the spirit-world is included in the cosmic words of the Seraphim, Cherubim and Thrones, is it again intoned in our humanity. It intones to us as human beings:

> In your worlds of will

>   Feel our cosmic working:
>
>   Spirit glows in matter,
>
>   When we create thinking;
>
>   Spirit creates in matter
>
>   When we willing live;
>
>   World *is* I-Willing Spirit-Word.

The world *is* the spirit-word which wills the I; and the world *is* in the creation by Seraphim, Cherubim and Thrones.

[This fourth stanza is written on the blackboard.]

> *Thrones, Cherubim, Seraphim:*
>
> *In your worlds of will*
>
> *Feel our cosmic working:*
>
> *Spirit glows in matter,*
>
> *When we create thinking;*
>
> *Spirit creates in matter*
>
> *When we willing live;*
>
> *World* is *I-Willing Spirit-Word.*

The spirit-word, which wills the I, *is* the world. And as we hear with the spiritual ear these words directed at our humanity, it becomes light in the spiritual world. The mild light which was there before is transformed into spiritual brightness.

This is the experience with the Guardian while the spiritual sphere is becoming light:

>   See the ether-rainbow arc's
>
>   Light teeming round,
>
>   Let the light creating force
>
>   Pass through your eyes,
>
>   Your I penetrate the circle,

Observe from the other side's vantage point

Color flooding the cosmic bowl.

Sense our thoughts

Breathing the colors of life

To the light-flooded bowl;

We carry the mirage of the senses

To spirit's domain of being

And turn, by the world inspired,

To serve the higher spirits.

What is received by you

From dead illusion made live:

We awaken it to existence;

We give it to the rays,

Who manifest with love

The nothingness of matter

In the spirit's essence.

In your worlds of will

Feel our cosmic working:

Spirit glows in matter,

When we create thinking;

Spirit creates in matter

When we willing live;

World *is* I-Willing Spirit-Word.

And it is as though the Guardian of the Threshold were touching us softly with his spiritual hands. We feel his presence as if he closed our spirit-eyes and we saw nothing for a moment, despite having been in a bright spiritual space a moment before. Words arise within me which I will place at the end of the lesson, to be saved for next time; I do not wish to include them as a mantra for today.

When the Guardian of the Threshold – if we may express with a sense-perceptible picture what takes place in a purely spiritual way – softly places his hands over our eyes so that we do not see the spiritual light around us, something arises in us that acts as a remembrance of the sensory world, which we had left behind in order to acquire knowledge in the spiritual world:

> I walked in this world of senses,
>
> Thought's legacy with me leading,
>
> A god's force had led me in.
>
> Death stands at the path's end.
>
> I will to feel the presence of Christ.
>
> In matter's death wakes the spirit's birth.
>
> Thus In spirit I find the world
>
> And know myself in the evolving world.

*

My dear friends, I must remind you of something I said upon the opening of these Class Lessons, and also during the Christmas Conference. It cannot be assumed that things which have been organized in a certain way for good reason may be changed from outside and be organized in a different way. Therefore I must announce here that in the future no application to the Class will be considered which is not directed to the secretary of the Executive Committee of the Goetheanum, Dr. Wegman, or directly to me. Only applications for participation in the Class Lessons directed to either one of these two will be considered. What has been the rule from the beginning must be continued. The members have not followed this procedure, but have done as they wish. And those who are already members of the Class should make this clear to others who want to participate.

On this occasion I would like to bring to your attention something else, my dear friends, which is especially grave now when the importance of how the Anthroposophical Society is managed must be maintained. Again and again letters are arriving which state: If I don't receive a reply, I will assume the answer to be affirmative. Those who have written in this way know who they are. I wish to inform those who have written in this way, and those who intend to do so, to please know that every letter which contains the sentence: I consider no answer to mean yes – that every such letter can form its own answer as being a negative. In the future such letters will not be answered, because one cannot accept such impertinence, but what is written in such letters must be regarded as containing their own rejection.

LESSON EIGHTEEN

Dornach, July 12, 1924

My dear Friends,
The call to self-knowledge, which the human soul can hear when it objectively pays attention to all the beings and events in nature and spiritual life, will pass before our souls again at the beginning of our considerations.

> O man, know thyself!
> So resounds the Cosmic-Word.
> You hear it strong in soul,
> You feel it firm in spirit.
>
> Who speaks with such cosmic might?
> Who speaks with such depth of heart?
>
> Does it work through distant radiant space
> Into your senses' sense of being?
> Does it ring through weaving waves of time
> Into your life's evolving stream?
>
> It's you yourself who,
> In feeling space, in experiencing time,
>
> The Word create, feeling foreign
> In the soulless void of space
> Because you lose the force of thought
> In time's destructive flow.

On the path to the answer which the soul can find to this question, my dear sisters and brothers, we have followed the path leading to the Guardian of the Threshold, to the abyss of being. We have progressed to where the Guardian of the Threshold instructs us so that what was previously dark and gloomy – although we knew that it contained the source of our being – expanded and became light. And then, in the increasing light, we heard the Guardian's call:

> See the ether-rainbow arc's
> Light teeming round,
> Let the light creating force
> Pass through your eyes,
> Your I penetrate the circle,
> Observe from the other side's vantage point
> Color flooding the cosmic bowl.

And the voices of the Angeloi, Archangeloi, Archai are intoned with these words as they are directed to the human souls:

> Sense our thoughts
> Breathing the colors of life
> To the light-flooded bowl;
> We carry the mirage of the senses
> To spirit's domain of being
> And turn, by the world inspired
> To serve the higher spirits.

And we see how through the flooding light in the cosmic bowl, which we met in the last lesson, the beings of the third hierarchy illuminate and are illuminated; we see the multitudes of these beings, Angeloi, Archangeloi, Archai, turn to the higher spirits, which they serve, to the Exusiai, Dynamis, Kyriotetes; and we are witnesses to how the Exusiai, Dynamis, Kyriotetes tell their serving spirits to fulfill the needs of human beings.

> The Exusiai, Dynamis, Kyriotetes speak:
>
> What you have received
> From dead illusion made live:
> We waken it to existence;
> We give it to the rays,
> Who manifest with love
> The nothingness of matter
> In the spirit's essence.

And then – impelled from within – we must turn our gaze to the highest spirits, the first hierarchy, who now turn to humanity in blessing. From them we hear:

> In the willing of your worlds
> Feel *our* world working:
> Spirit glows in matter
> When, thinking, we create.
> Spirit creates in matter
> When we live in willing:
> World *is* the I-willing Spirit-Word.

As witnesses to how the beings of the higher worlds speak to each other, so penetrated with what the highest beings let stream into human souls as the cosmic-word so that the human heart may resonate with it, we must feel ourselves to be within the all-moving, all-pervading cosmic light in which we ourselves live and move.

And now we come to a truth, which is perceived where the non-embodied beings live, where the spirits live their lives, where the spirits think their truths, where the spirits radiate their beauty, where their spiritual acts take place. And we recognize the greatness, the all-pervading, weaving truth in the spirit-worlds: *spirit is*. For we are, we live, we act in spirit. We perceive spiritual being.

And now we realize that spirit, in which we now live, alone *is*. We now know that even here, in the world of sensory illusion, is only spirit. Only spirit *is*. This stands before our souls as unshakable, all-pervading truth: spirit *is*. And we do well to place this truth before our souls in picture form.

[Drawing on the blackboard: red]

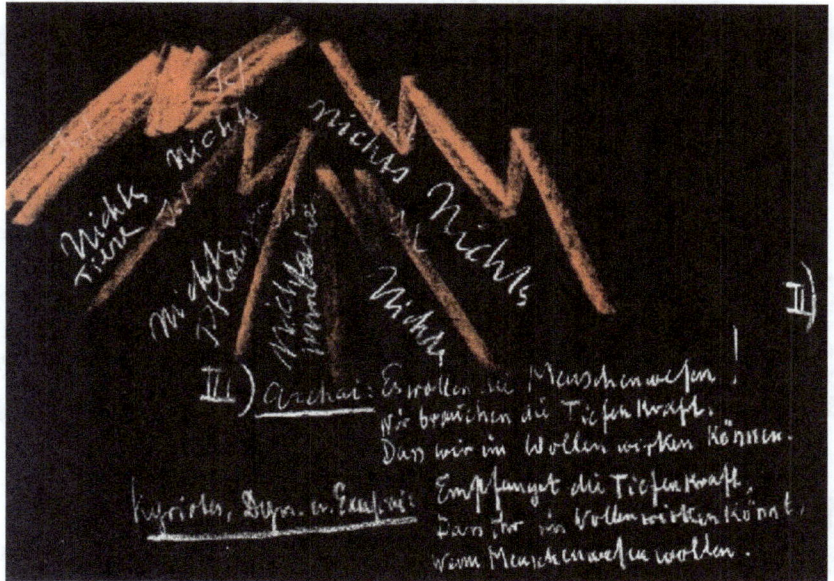

Blackboard Drawing for Lesson Eighteen

What is expressed here in the drawing is spirit. It is spirit alone.

[While continuing to speak, Rudolf Steiner inserts the word "*Ist*" in the red lines of the drawing – barely visible here.]

What is here: *Is* – is spirit. And what is outside this red is nothing. This is placed before our souls. And the spirit-world tells us [pointing]: here *Is*, here *Is*, here *Is*. Everywhere that spirit is, *Is* something.

[As he continues to speak, Rudolf Steiner writes the word *Nichts* (nothing) in various places between the read lines, then the worlds *Mineralien* (minerals), *Pflanzen* (plants), *Tiere* (animals).]

And where there is no spirit, there is *nothing*. We are profoundly impressed by this truth: Everywhere where spirit is, is something, and where there is no spirit, is *nothing*. And now we wonder: How did all this seem to us there in the world of sensory illusion, which we left to enter the spiritual world, where we find true being, the spirit revealed to our souls. Over there we did not see what is drawn here in red. We are too weak there to see what is drawn here in red. What remains there then? *Nothing*. Over there we see

Nothing, call it *minerals*, one kind of Nothing; call it *plants*, a second kind of Nothing; call it animals, a third kind of Nothing, and so forth.

We see Nothing because we are too weak to see Something. And we call the Nothings the kingdoms of nature. That is the great deception, the great illusion. Over there only variations of the Nothing are visible when we look out from the body. And we feel deeply the impression, as we live over there and give names to what is fundamentally Nothing, that it is the great illusion. And what is Nothing, and what we give names to now appears to us as the sum of names which we give to Nothingness. For in their reality all beings are only present in the spiritual world that we have now entered. Names dedicated to Nothing we have wasted on the non-existent. And beings – not those from the domains of the gods to which we belong and to which we should belong – can take possession of the names which we have wasted on the Nothings. And they keep these names from now on.

If we are not clear about the fact that here on earth we give names to nullities, we fall with our nullities into the greatest illusion. We must know that we are giving names to the nullities. It is now clear to us, because over there [in the spirit-world] we live and move in the light, and the spiritual strength of our hearts has remained there, we can feel deeply, deeply, deeply: We now know that we have gone from the kingdom of illusions to the kingdom of truth. Earnestness, holy earnestness in respect to the truth begins to act in our souls.

And now we look back at the faithful Guardian of the Threshold, who stands at the abyss of being. He doesn't speak now. He spoke from out of the darkness. He spoke when we first felt the brightness. He spoke when the darkness [in the stenography "brightness" - possibly an error.] was brightening for us. Now, as we stand shaken by the great truth "only spirit *is*", he stands there speechless, pointing above to where the beings of the higher hierarchies speak to each other. And with presence of mind we think for a moment: Below in earthly life we perceived the impression made on us by minerals, by plants, by animals, by physical human beings; we heard what the clouds say, what the mountains say, how the fountains ripple, how the lightning flashes, how the thunder rolls, what the stars whisper about cosmic secrets. That was our experience down below. Now beyond the abyss of existence all that is silent. Now we are witnesses to the gods speaking to each other. The whole choir of Angeloi begins to speak.

We look up and see how the choir turns to the spirits of the second hierarchy, which they wish to serve. We observe the loving, serving gestures of the Angeloi, Archangeloi, Archai, who turn to the Exusiai, Dynamis, Kyriotetes. We view the serving multitudes of the third hierarchy.

We view the multitudes of the second hierarchy in world-creation, in world-dominion, in world-illumination, and we hear what the spiritual-illuminating, divine-willing beings speak to each other.

We hear the Angeloi intoning their words of concern for the guidance of human souls. Their words resonate:

The human beings think!

This weighs on the Angeloi. They are concerned as to how they should guide human souls, because humans think. Then they turn to the Dynamis for the force needed to guide human beings in their thinking.

> Angeloi:
> The human beings think!
> We need the light from the heights
> That we may illuminate their thinking.

From the realm of radiance, dominion, acting, the Dynamis lovingly and benevolently reply:

> Receive the light from the heights,
> So you can illuminate thought,
> When human beings think.

And the flooding light, the force of illumination in thought, streams over from the Dynamis to the Angeloi. What the Angeloi receive enlightens, without our knowing, human thinking. Now we realize what acts and weaves in human thinking: the illumination of the Angeloi. But the light force for this illumination they receive from the Dynamis.

[The first part of the mantra is written on the blackboard. Italics indicate writing.]

> II Angeloi:
> "Human being think!": their concern is expressed in their words.
> *Human beings think!*
> They turn to the Dynamis with their concern:
> *We need the light from the heights*
> *That we may illuminate their thinking.*
>
> The Dynamis reply:
> *Dynamis:*
> *Receive the light from the heights,*
> *So you can illuminate thought,*
> *When human beings think.*

Our spiritual view goes farther. We see the multitude of Archangeloi turning to the second hierarchy. They turn to the Exusiai and Kyriotetes, to two categories of spirits of the second hierarchy. (The Angeloi had turned to the Dynamis: Archangeloi turn to the Exusiai and Kyriotetes.) Their concern is for human beings' feeling. And they request from the Exusiai and Kyriotetes what they need in order to guide human beings in their feeling.

> Archangeloi:
> The human beings feel!

> We need warmth of soul,
> That we may live in feeling.

They must breathe life into feeling. And with powerful voices, because two choirs are answering, Kyriotetes and Exusiai voices ring out in the spiritual cosmos:

> Receive warmth of soul
> That you may live in feeling
> When human beings feel.

[The second part of the mantra is written on the blackboard.]

> *II) Archangeloi:*
> *The human beings feel!*
> *We need warmth of soul,*
> *That we may live in feeling.*
>
> *The reply:*
> *Kyriotetes and Exusiai:*
> *Receive warmth of soul*
> *That you may live in feeling*
> *When human beings feel.*

We turn to the third multitude of the third hierarchy, to the Archai. They have concern for the will of the human being, the third concern of the third hierarchy.

We feel: when the Angeloi turn to the Dynamis, then the Dynamis act way up in the heights in order to give the light they create from the heights to the Angeloi for their concern for human thinking. And we feel: everything in the compass of cosmic warmth is created by the Exusiai and Kyriotetes, and it is given over to the Archangeloi so that they can guide human feeling. And deep below, where the spirits and gods of the depths prevail, and where from the abysses – in which much evil moves – the good forces of the deep must be drawn up high, so all the gods of the second hierarchy pull together; for in their concern for the human being´s will, the Archai need the forces of the deep. They speak:

> The human beings will!
> We need the forces of the depths,
> That we may work in willing.

And the powerful spirits of the second hierarchy answer with a mighty cosmic voice in the combined voices of all three together, the three choirs forming one choir – Kyriotetes, Dynamis, Exusiai – three choirs in one:

> Receive the force of the depths,
> That you may work in willing,
> When human beings will.

[The third part of the mantra is written on the blackboard.]

> *III) Archai:*
> *The human beings will!*
> *We need the forces of the depths,*
> *That we may work in willing.*

Kyriotetes, Dynamis and Exusiai answer together:

> *Kyriotetes, Dynamis and Exusiai:*
> *Receive the force of the depths,*
> *That you may work in willing,*
> *When human beings will.*

This is the world, existing in the holy words of creation, of which we will be witnesses in spiritual worlds, as we are witnesses of the events in the mineral and vegetable kingdoms here in earth.

And we hear, in that it becomes our experience:

> The human beings think!
> We need the light from the heights
> That we may illuminate their thinking.

> Receive the light from the heights,
> So you can illuminate thought,
> When human beings think.

> The human beings feel!
> We need warmth of soul,
> That we may live in feeling.

> Receive warmth of soul
> That you may live in feeling
> When human beings feel.

> The human beings will!
> We need the forces of the depths,
> That we may work in willing.

> Receive the force of the depths,
> That you may work in willing,
> When human beings will.

We grow into the spiritual world. Instead of what surrounds us here in the sensory earth, the choirs of the spiritual world surround us. And we become witnesses to what the gods say in their creative concern for the world of humans.

Only when in our meditation we go on to the complete elimination of what we are here on earth, and to having a feeling for the world the gods are forming with their divine speech, do we experience true reality. And only when we possess this reality, do we also know what really surrounds us between birth and death. Because behind the appearances in life between birth and death is the reality of what we experience between death and rebirth.

In earlier times people living on earth had a dull, dreamlike clairvoyance. Their souls were filled with dreamlike pictures, spoken [sic] from the spiritual world. Let us imagine a person from olden times. When he was not working, and was resting – although the sun was still in the sky – and was thinking back, pictures arose which he experienced in his soul and which reminded him of what he had experienced in pre-earthly existence in the spiritual world. But he didn't understand the connection between his earthly existence and that existence which shone into his clairvoyant dreams. But the initiates and their teachings were there. They explained the connection, first to their students, and through their students to all the people. So they lived in the earthly world experiencing the memories of pre-earthly existence.

Nowadays in earthly life the memory of pre-earthly existence has been extinguished. Initiates cannot explain the connection between earthly life and pre-earthly existence, because humans have forgotten what they experienced in pre-earthly existence. Such an explanation is not possible because the cosmic memory no longer exists.

Nevertheless, what the gods are saying behind sensory being must be heard by means of initiation-science. Human beings must experience it. And soon the time will come – it's approaching more and more – when a person who passes through the gate of death will only be able to understand the spiritual world into which he enters if he realizes that when a person enters heavenly existence through the gate of death, and finds himself in the reality of the spiritual worlds, within the world of Angeloi, Archangeloi, Archai, Exusiai, Dynamis, Kyriotetes, Seraphim, Cherubim, Thrones – if he experiences all this, if what he experiences after death it is not to remain incomprehensible and dark to him, then he will have to remember what he experienced here on earth through initiation-science.

And what is extremely important in understanding what can be experienced in life between death and a new birth – if it has been heard, otherwise it cannot be understood – is remembrance of what is still heard on earth, and which resounds as follows:

> The human beings think!
> Receive the light from the heights.
>
> The human beings feel!
> Receive warmth of soul.
>
> The human beings will!
> Receive the force of the depths.

These, my sisters and brothers, are the words that should be heard today in the esoteric schools. They should resound through the instructions of those who lead the esoteric schools with the force of the Michael age. Then it can be thus:

In the esoteric schools the voice of the Angeloi are first heard within the earthly sphere:

> The human beings think!
> The Dynamis' reply:
> Receive the light of the heights.
>
> The voice of the Archangeloi is heard:
> The human beings feel!
> The reply of the Kyriotetes and Exusiai:
> Receive the warmth of soul.
>
> The Archai's words:
> The human beings will!

The answer of all three members of the second hierarchy – Exusiai, Dynamis, Kyriotetes:
Receive the force of the depths.

Those people who have heard those words in esoteric schools will go through the gate of death, where they will again hear all these words resounding together: the esoteric schools here, life between death and a new birth there. They will understand what is resonating there.

Or they will be dull and unwilling – after preparation by general anthroposophy – in respect to what is said in the esoteric schools. They do not perceive what can be heard through initiation-science from the realm of the heights. They go through the gate of death. They hear there what they should already have heard here. They don't understand it. When the gods speak to each other with powerful words, it sounds to them like incomprehensible ringing, mere sounds, cosmic noise.

Paul speaks about this in the Gospel – that through the teachings of Christ men should protect themselves from death in the spirit-land. For death soon comes in the spirit-land if we go through the gate of death and don't understand what is resonating there, if we can only hear the incomprehensible sounds instead of the understandable words of the gods, because we have been overcome by the soul's death instead of the soul's life. There is an initiation-science because souls are alive. There are esoteric schools so that souls may remain alive when they go through the gate of death. This we must feel deeply [1].

And now let us consider the path we have taken in spirit, how we approached the Guardian in order to learn how the human being crosses the abyss of existence. And let us also consider how the impressions there acted on our souls; let us take into our souls the inner drama of self-knowledge.

We have traveled the path. Three tablets stood there, so to speak. We are now standing before the third one, after we have taken into our souls all the profundities of divine speech. On the first tablet, long before we arrived at the abyss of existence, resonated:

> O man, know thyself!
> So resounds the Cosmic-Word.
> You hear it strong in soul,
> You feel it firm in spirit.
>
> Who speaks with such cosmic might?
> Who speaks with such depth of heart?
>
> Does it work through distant radiant space
> Into your senses' sense of being?
> Does it ring through weaving waves of time
> Into your life's evolving stream?
>
> It's you yourself who,
> In feeling space, in experiencing time
>
> The Word create, feeling foreign
> In the soulless void of space,
> Because you lose the force of thought
> In time's destructive flow.

Then we approached the Guardian. The second tablet stands there. On it stands:

> Recognize first the earnest Guardian,
> Who stands before the gates of spirit-land,
> Denying entrance of your sensory force
> And your power of understanding,
> For in your sensory weaving
> And in creation of your thoughts,
> From space's emptiness,
> From the illusion of time's might,
> You must first forcefully seize
> The truth of your own being.

We have arrived on the other side, passing the earnest Guardian, and have heard a conversation such as this:

> The human beings think!
> Receive the light of the heights.
>
> The human beings feel!

> Receive the warmth of soul.
>
> The human beings will!
> Receive the force of the depths.

We look back to the world of senses and we feel about this sensory world the words:

> I entered in this world of senses,
> Bearing with me thinking's legacy,
> A godly force led me in.
> Death stands at the path's end.
> I will to feel the being of Christ.
> In matter's death he wakens spirit-birth.
> Thus in spirit I find the world
> And know myself in world-becoming

[1] In a previous paragraph leading up to these words, Rudolf Steiner says: "*And soon the time will come – it's approaching more and more – when a person who passes through the gate of death will only be able to understand the spiritual world into which he enters if ...*" (Und immer mehr wird die Zeit kommen...) which seems to indicate that this means sometime in the future. [Ed./Trans.]

LESSON NINETEEN

Dornach, August 2, 1924

My dear friends,

Again we shall let the verse flow through our souls which can bring to mind how everything that is, was in the past and will be in the future, calls out to us to seek self-knowledge, for it is the foundation of all real, true cosmic knowledge.

> O man, know thyself!
> So resounds the Cosmic-Word.
> You hear it strong in soul,
> You feel it firm in spirit.
>
> Who speaks with such cosmic might?
> Who speaks with such depth of heart?
>
> Does it work through distant radiant space
> Into your senses' sense of being?
> Does it ring through weaving waves of time
> Into your life's evolving stream?
>
> It's you yourself who,
> In feeling space, in experiencing time,
>
> The Word create, feeling foreign
> In the soulless void of space
> Because you lose the force of thought
> In time's destructive flow.

My dear sisters and brothers, we have let mantric verses pass into our souls which, through their force, contain the path into spirit-land, first passing the Guardian of the Threshold into what is at first a dark, gloomy, night-engulfed spiritual world, where light is felt, which then becomes light for our spiritual perception. We have seen in this spiritual world how the human being participates – usually unconsciously, though he can be conscious of it – in the dialogs of the higher hierarchies – as though the Cosmic Word itself were acting together with the higher hierarchies. And finally we have been able to move on to the cosmic realm where the choruses of the different hierarchies resound together. Let us now bring that to mind once more – how we had already continued from hearing what the beings of the second hierarchy were saying to where the beings of the first hierarchy speak. And now we are able to hear them speaking in harmony as a chorus.

The Guardian brings it to our attention; we know this from previous lessons:

> See the ether-rainbow arc's
>
> Light teeming round,
>
> Let the light-creating force
>
> Pass through your eyes,
>
> Your I penetrate the circle,
>
> Observe from the other side's vantage point
>
> Color flooding the cosmic bowl.

After the Guardian reveals to us this spiritual secret of the rainbow, from the chorus of the Angeloi, Archangeloi and Archai we hear resound:

> Sense our thoughts
>
> Breathing the colors of life
>
> Into the light-flooded bowl;
>
> We carry the mirage of the senses
>
> To spirit's domain of being
>
> And turn, by the world inspired,
>
> To serve the higher spirits.

The spirits of the third hierarchy explain how they wish to serve the spirits of the second hierarchy for the benefit of humanity: we hear again the Exusiai, Dynamis, Kyriotetes in chorus from their realm:

> What you have received
>
> From dead illusion made live:
>
> We waken it to existence;
>
> We give it to the rays,
>
> Who manifest with love
>
> The nothingness of matter
>
> In the spirit's being.

And once we have heard how the beings of the second hierarchy, creating the world, approach our I; then the choir of the first hierarchy resounds – the Thrones, Seraphim and Cherubim:

> In the willing of your worlds
>
> Feel *our* world working:
>
> Spirit glows in matter
>
> When, thinking, we create.
>
> Spirit creates in matter
>
> When we live in willing:
>
> World *is* the I-willing Spirit-Word.

Now we stand within the Spirit-Word, the Spirit-Word that underlies the creation of the world. We feel ourselves surrounded by this Spirit-Word. We feel the world penetrated by this Spirit-Word. We feel ourselves woven within this Spirit-Word. We feel it penetrating into our humanity. Finally we feel this cosmic Spirit-Word streaming into our hearts; we feel our whole humanity immersed in the waves of this Spirit-Word. We feel ourselves spiritually immersed in the spiritual world interwoven with the Word.

The Guardian is there in the distance. We had passed him by. He is now far in the distance. We now hear him as he softly speaks a last word of warning to our spirit-ear from afar. The Guardian speaks:

> Who speaks in the Spirit-Word
>
> With the voice
>
> Which blazes in the cosmic fire?

From the realm of the first hierarchy comes the answer:

> The flame of the stars speaks,
>
> Seraphic Fire-Forces flame;
>
> They flame also in my heart.
>
> In the primal being's fount of love
>
> The human heart finds

Creative spirit-flaming-speech:

It is I.

My dear sisters and brothers, if we wish to enter the esoteric realm, we should first feel that the ancient holy "'eyeh 'asher 'eyeh!" – "I am I", "I am" is a holy word which resounds from that other worldly reality. What our fleeting thoughts understand as "I am" is only a reflection of it.

We must be aware that the true "I am" does not come from us in the earthly realm, that if we wish to say "I am" worthily, we must first enter the realm of the Seraphim, Cherubim and Thrones. Only there does "I am" sound true. Here in the earthly realm it is illusion.

In order to experience the true "I am" within us, we must hear the Cosmic-Word. So we must listen to the Guardian of the Threshold's question: who speaks in the Cosmic-Word? Seraphim, who wend their way through the cosmic waves with spiritual flames of lightning, where we now stand. The Word is flame, a flaming voice. And in experiencing ourselves in this blazing cosmic fire, which speaks the fire language in the flaming fire, we experience the true "I am".

This is contained in the Guardian of the Threshold's question posed from the distance – we have passed him long ago – and the answer comes from the realm of the first hierarchy:

> Who speaks in the Spirit-Word
>
> With the voice
>
> Which blazes in the cosmic fire?
>
> The flame of the stars speaks,
>
> Seraphic fire-forces flaming;
>
> They flame also in my heart.
>
> In the primal being's fount of love
>
> The human heart finds
>
> Creative spirit-speech aflame:
>
> It is I.

[The first part of the mantra is written on the blackboard:]

The Guardian speaks from afar (The human-I knows itself to be in the realm of Spirit-Word borne by the Seraphim, Cherubim, Thrones):

> *Who speaks in the Spirit-Word*
>
> *With the voice*
>
> *Which blazes in the cosmic fire?*

Again the answer comes to us from the realm of the first hierarchy:

> *The flame of the stars speaks,*
>
> *Seraphic fire-forces flaming;*
>
> *They flame also in my heart.*
>
> *In the primal being's fount of love*
>
> *The human heart finds*
>
> *Creative spirit-speech aflame:*
>
> *It is I.*

When human words resound, then human thinking speaks through human words. When the spirit's cosmic-word resounds, then cosmic thinking speaks through the spirit's cosmic-word. This lies in the Guardian's second question, which he now poses from afar.

The Guardian speaks from afar. The human-I knows itself to be in the realm of the Spirit-Word borne by the Seraphim, Cherubim, Thrones:

> *What thinks in the Spirit-Word*
>
> *With thoughts*
>
> *Which are formed from cosmic souls?*

They are the thoughts that come from all the cosmic souls, which belong to the beings of the various hierarchies. They form and shape everything in the kingdoms of the world. Therefore the Guardian asks who thinks the formative forces:

> What thinks in the Spirit-Word
>
> With thoughts
>
> Which are formed from cosmic souls?

Again from the realm of the first hierarchy the answer comes to us:

> The glow of the stars thinks.

First it was the flames that speak the words; the star-flames speak the words. The glow that come from the flames thinks.

> The glow of the stars thinks,
>
> The formative forces of the Cherubim glow;
>
> They also glow in my head.

This is what the human being who stands within it all says.

> In the primal beings' source of light
>
> The human head finds
>
> Thinking soul-forming at work:
>
> It is I.

This is the second dialog – as though the beings of the first hierarchy were giving us cosmic permission to experience the "I am":

> What thinks in the Spirit-Word
>
> With thoughts
>
> Which are formed from cosmic souls?

> The glow of the stars thinks,
>
> The formative forces of the Cherubim glow;

> They also glow in my head.
>
> In the primal beings' source of light
>
> The human head finds
>
> Thinking soul-forming at work:
>
> It is I.

[The second part of the mantra is written on the blackboard.]

> *The Guardian speaks from afar:*
> *What thinks in the Spirit-Word*
> *With thoughts*
> *Which are formed from cosmic souls?*
>
> *From the realm of the first hierarchy:*
>
> *The glow of the stars thinks,*
> *The formative forces of the Cherubim glow;*
> *They also glow in my head.*
> *In the primal beings' source of light*
> *The human head finds*
> *Thinking soul-forming at work:*
> *It is I.*

The cosmic Spirit-Word must speak. Thoughts stream from it. But the thoughts are creative; the thoughts are permeated with forces; the thoughts stream; and cosmic beings and cosmic events, everything which is evolves from them. In it, in the thought bearing Cosmic-Word live the word-created cosmic thoughts. It is not mere thinking, it is not mere speaking, it is force, forces streaming in the Words. Forces inscribe the thoughts into the cosmic beings, into the cosmic events.

Thereby the third question which the Guardian of the Threshold asks from afar is indicated:

> What impels in the Spirit-Word
>
> With forces
>
> Which live in the cosmic body?

The whole world, which resounds from the Cosmic-Word, which gleams from the cosmic-thoughts, is what thinks and speaks in humans, what bears the body, the thought pervaded cosmic body. The Thrones bear it, or rather the Thrones bear the thought illumined cosmic Spirit-Word that is within it.

Therefore the answer to the Guardian's question comes from the first hierarchy:

> The cosmic body of the stars impels,
>
> The Thrones' bearing powers "body".

We must form a picture which is otherwise unusual. But just as one "enlightens" from light, and can form the verb "to live" from life, so also can one form the word "to body" from the force used to bear the body. [1] For body is not dead, it is not something finished. Body is something which is active at every moment, mobile, alert, something that "bodies" ["leibt"].

> The Thrones' bearing powers embody.
>
> They also embody in my limbs.
>
> In the primal being's source of life
>
> Human limbs find
>
> Forceful Cosmic-bearer-powers.
>
> It is I.

Cosmic-Word, cosmic-thinking, cosmic-body; the speaking, thinking cosmic-body is what the Guardian's third question refers to:

> What impels in the Spirit-Word
>
> With forces
>
> Which live in the cosmic body?

> The cosmic body of the stars impels,
>
> The Thrones' bearing powers embody;
>
> They also embody in my limbs.
>
> In the primal being's source of life
>
> Human limbs find
>
> Forceful cosmic-bearer-powers.
>
> It is I.

[The third part of the mantra is written on the blackboard.]

> *The Guardian speaks from afar:*

— The human-I knows itself to be in the realm of the Spirit-Word borne by the Seraphim, Cherubim, Thrones —

> *What impels in the Spirit-Word*
>
> *With forces,*
>
> *Which live in the cosmic body?*

> *From the realm of the first hierarchy:*

> *The cosmic body of the stars impels,*
>
> *The Thrones' bearing powers embody;*
>
> *They also embody in my limbs.*
>
> *In the primal being's source of life*
>
> *Human limbs find*
>
> *Forceful Cosmic-bearer-powers.*
>
> *It is I.*

In a certain sense, my sisters and brothers, it is a kind of conclusion to the path that began in the realm of illusion, of maya, which led us to the Guardian of the Threshold, which led us to self-knowledge, and through self-knowledge over to the spiritual realm, and allowed us to hear the choirs of the hierarchies. In a certain sense it is a conclusion when we now stand at the place where we may experience in ourselves the true "I am", "'eyeh 'asher 'eyeh".

In this dialog we can experience, when the threefold "It is I" streams from the heart, where it may stream from the heart; when it streams from the heart in such a way that it is the echo of what resounds in these hearts from the Seraphim, Cherubim, Thrones:

> Who speaks in the Spirit-Word
>
> With the voice
>
> Which blazes in the cosmic fire?
>
> The flame of the stars speaks,
>
> Seraphic fire-forces flaming;
>
> They flame also in my heart.
>
> In the primal being's fount of love
>
> The human heart finds
>
> Creative spirit-speech aflame:
>
> It is I.
>
> What thinks in the Spirit-Word
>
> With thoughts
>
> Which are formed from cosmic souls?
>
> The glow of the stars thinks,
>
> The formative forces of the Cherubim glow;
>
> They also glow in my head.
>
> In the primal beings' source of light
>
> The human head finds
>
> Thinking soul-forming at work:
>
> It is I.

> What impels in the Spirit-Word
>
> With forces
>
> Which live in the cosmic body?
>
> The cosmic body of the stars impels,
>
> The Thrones' bearing powers embody;
>
> They also embody in my limbs.
>
> In the primal being's source of life
>
> Human limbs find
>
> Forceful Cosmic-bearer-powers.
>
> It is I.

Here, my dear sisters and brothers, in a certain sense we have completed the first section of this First Class of the School.

We have heard the communications which we have received from the spiritual worlds – for this School is one which has been constituted by the spiritual worlds themselves; we have let the images and inspirations which can come from the spiritual worlds pass through us. They point out to our souls the path to understanding the true Human I in the surroundings of the Seraphim, Cherubim, Thrones.

My dear sisters and brothers! It was, as you have heard in the general anthroposophical lectures, Michael's super-sensible School in which such inner heartfelt teachings first resounded. They were the powerful pictures of the imaginative ritual at the beginning of the nineteenth century, where the souls who were selected to be close to Michael were taught the School's revelations of the fifteenth, sixteenth, seventeenth centuries, and which was led by Michael and his companions in the way described here. And now we are here in this anthroposophical School founded by Michael. We feel ourselves to be in it. They are the words of Michael which were to characterize the path which leads into the spiritual world and the human I: The words of Michael. These words of Michael of the super-sensible Michael-School constituted the first section.

When in September we find ourselves again in these Class Lessons, it will be Michael's will to describe the imaginative ritual revelations of the beginning of the nineteenth century. [2] That will be the second section. What has been presented to us in mantric words, will stand before our souls as pictures, which will be – to the extent possible – the pictures of the super-sensible imaginative ritual brought down at the beginning of the nineteenth century.

The third stage of this School will consist of what will lead us directly to the interpretations of the mantric words that were given in the super-sensible Michael School of the fifteenth, sixteenth, seventeenth centuries.

*

We should feel how we ourselves go through all this in the spiritual world. We should always keep looking back to the physical-sensory world of the earth and humbly absorb everything that takes place in the physical-sensory world of the earth.

Therefore, in conclusion let resound on our souls again what – if we are capable of absorbing it and appreciating it – what resounds from every stone, from every plant, from every moving cloud, from every bubbling spring, from every rustling wind, from the forests and the mountains, everywhere from the things and events that resound from the earthly sphere, if we are appreciative of it.

We were in the realm of the Seraphim, Cherubim, Thrones. Even the Guardian of the Threshold only called from afar. We go back again with humility, past the Guardian, out to the realm of sensory appearances. And again we let these words resound in us:

> O man, know thyself!
> So resounds the Cosmic-Word.
> You hear it strong in soul,
> You feel it firm in spirit.
>
> Who speaks with such cosmic might?
> Who speaks with such depth of heart?
>
> Does it work through distant radiant space
> Into your senses' sense of being?
> Does it ring through weaving waves of time
> Into your life's evolving stream?
>
> It's you yourself who,
> In feeling space, in experiencing time,
>
> The Word create, feeling foreign
> In the soulless void of space
> Because you lose the force of thought
> In time's destructive flow.

*

My dear sisters and brothers, it is unfortunately the case that the measures, which have been repeated sufficiently within this Esoteric School, have been observed in a strange way by many who have become members by requesting membership and attained it; and just yesterday I had to criticize some rather unedifying matters. It is hard to believe, but it is really the case that members have left their blue membership certificates here on the chairs to reserve their places. It has also happened that three members have left notebooks – one folder and two notebooks – have been simply left lying around. The folder with the typewritten verses was found out on the street. From one of the notebooks could be copied what I told you yesterday. Another notebook was left lying in the Glasshaus. Therefore it was necessary to expel three members of this School directly before this Class Lesson began.

With these, there have been nineteen expulsions from the School. One could have expected that earnestness would mean more to those who have already heard here what this School means. One of them loses the verses on the street, another leaves them lying here, the third leaves them lying in the Glasshaus: so it was necessary to expel three quite prominent members of the School. And I can assure you, my dear sisters and brothers, that the strict observance of rules I informed you of at the beginning and often repeated, must be strictly observed. Such a School with the esoteric earnestness can only be maintained if its members really observe what is demanded in the name of the spiritual powers which direct it.

With true occult matters it is really so. And what has been often occurring in the Anthroposophical Society can no longer continue. That which is filled with earnestness by its own character, must also be treated with earnestness.

---

[1] The verb "leiben" – "to body" – does not exist in German or English. Here Rudolf Steiner invents the word, so to speak. There is a subtle difference between the two German words which mean "body": *Leib* and *Körper*. In the theological sense *Leib* indicates a kind of soul function which the biological concept of *Körper* lacks. Because there is only one word in English for body, I feel justified in using "embody", where Steiner said "to body" or "bodies" which are so awkward in English, as they are in German. But embody does follow his line of thought deriving "enlighten" from "light", for example. If someone wishes to stick closely to the literal translation, he/she may substitute "to body" or "bodies" where "embody" or "embodies" appears.

[2] Due to the great increase in new Class members, the announced second section could not begin in September of 1924. Instead, repetition classes were held. These will be the contents of Volume III. Due to Rudolf Steiner's premature death in March of 1925, the Esoteric School Classes were left incomplete.

Rudolf Steiner Portrait
by Peter Gospodinov

Peter Gospodinov was born in 1974. During the period, 1994 – 1997, he attended the Art Academy Sofia, BG. During the period, 1999 – 2003, he attended the Visual Art School in Basel. For more information on Peter, use this URL: https://www.petergos.com/

RUDOLF STEINER